RADIO 270

The zany team of DJ's ready for the Summer 66 launch.

RADIO 270

Life on the Oceaan waves

The incredible story of Yorkshire's own Offshore Radio Station

On-Air 1966 - 1967

BOB PREEDY

Based on personal interviews with Leonard Dale, Peter Duncan, Stella Ellis, Wilf Proudfoot and Don Robinson.

A Broadcasting History book
published by
R.E.Preedy
Wetherby LS22 6WG

Copyright 2002
ISBN 1 8743660 2 0

All rights reserved
No reproduction in any form unless with written
permission from the publisher

Printed in the UK by
The Amadeus Press, Cleckheaton

Previous Books

Leeds Cinemas Remembered.

Leeds Theatres Remembered.

Harrogate Cinemas & Theatres.

Leeds Cinemas 2.

The Cinemas of Bradford.

The Cinemas of Humberside.

Flick - Cinemas in Leeds & Bradford.

That'll be The Day in Leeds.

Roller Coasters - Their Amazing History.

Roller Coasters - Shake Rattle & Roll.

West Yorkshire (Francis Frith).

Ilkley.

Yorkshire - A Second Selection.

TUESDAY, OCTOBER 12, 1965

Radio Yorks on the air off Brid in February

GOING on the air in February next year will be Radio Yorkshire, a new "pirate" radio ship which, it is claimed, will reach about 10,000,000 people in an area ranging from Newcastle-on-Tyne to Leicester. Behind the venture is Scarborough businessman Mr. Don Robinson, of Robinson's Promotions Ltd.

Mr. Robinson said today that had already obtained the tran equipment

Contents

Introduction

Chapter One — **Something's In the Air - 1965**

Chapter Two — **The Key Players**

Chapter Three — **My Ship is Coming In**

Chapter Four — **The Countdown to Broadcasting**

Chapter Five — **Eventually On-Air 1966 Month by Month**

Chapter Six — **On-Air 1967 Month by Month**

Chapter Seven — **The End of Broadcasting - August**

Chapter Eight — **The End of the Ship - Oceaan 7**

Chapter Nine — **The Dream of Land-Based Radio**

Chapter Ten — **The DJs - Where Are They Now?**

About the Author

Introduction

There are few books covering the subject of broadcasting. Even fewer give much space to Radio 270.
Based in the north and coming onto the air fairly late in the pirate radio era, the history of the Yorkshire coast's only offshore station is sketchy and repetitive at best.

I first became interested in the station when as a teenager in Derbyshire I used our TV aerial to drag in the new pop stations on my transistor radio. Like many thousands of others I tuned in vain to find Radio 270 on April 1st 1966, oblivious to the offshore drama unfolding near Scarborough.

Eventually when it did begin transmitting in June a certain sparkle had gone but the mystique remained. The early shows were full of good northern fun and Yorkshire bluntness. It even became exciting to drive through Seamer and see a Proudfoot supermarket!

Life on the station could never be called boring. Its transmitter broke down often and the chat between the discs was frequently hilarious and embarrassing - but it remained "our" station in the north.

After the offshore stations closed in 1967 it was a real loss to a new generation of freedom loving teenagers. I kept hoping a book about Radio 270 would appear. Perhaps by the 10th anniversary? Sadly no - and 20, 30, and 35 years went by and still nothing!

So I began my research. And here is that amazing story full of intrigue, boardroom battles, overpowering Programme

Directors, technical disasters and DJ mutinies. Many shareholders and directors of 270 were happy to tell me about their part in the jigsaw. Surprisingly though, considering talk is their trade, a number of the DJs were initially reluctant to reminisce about their role on the station.

Perhaps Leonard Dale, Chairman of Radio 270, put the whole project in perspective when he told me : -

"Radio 270 was perfectly legal, unlike the rest of the stations around Britain. Everything which was done on Radio 270 was done legally, and the company was properly constituted as a foreign company transmitting outside Britain. What put us off the air was that the government made it illegal for anyone to take advertising on our station, or it was illegal for anyone to supply us with food. These laws came out purely to put Radio 270 off the air. The other stations could have been put off air at any single time that the Government had wished.

Quite frankly the Radio 270 period is a period of my business life which I want to forget. It did do one useful thing, and that was it gave me a very good understanding of the cesspool operations of the entertainment world."

After that I definitely wanted to know more....

So relive those days, but spare a thought for those who had to sound cheerful during a gut-wrenching force 10 gale off the exposed north-east coast!

Bob Preedy
Wetherby
April 2002

Robinson's Promotions Limited

managing director - Don Robinson   general manager - T. H. Hanson
secretary - D. R. Cox, A.C.A.

Sports & Entertainments
Closed Circuit Television
Sports Promoters

head office: Westminster Bank Chambers, St. Nicholas Street, Scarborough

Telephone - Scarborough 701/2   Telegrams - "Wrestling, Scarborough"

DR/MJH

Mr. P. Duncan,
9 Woodlands Court,
TROCKLEY ON TYNE.   25th October, 1965

Dear Peter,

    You will be pleased to learn that we are now going to purchase a boat in Holland. This is a much more modern boat than I had in mind at first, in fact it has a diesal engine so instead of costing around about £250 per week in fuel, this is now down to £20, as you see a great saving.

    It is important for you to come down this week as early as possible to discuss this with Bill Pashby the boat expert remember who you met. Could you arrange to stay the night as we have a number of things to talk over.

    I think also that Bill would like you to fly over to Holland with him the week after next to show him what alterations you need for the boat. This will mean flying out one day and returning the next.

    I am also in touch with an American to come over for a year to act as programme controller.

                        Yours sincerely,

                          Don Robinson,
                          DON ROBINSON'S PROMOTIONS LTD.

Any offer contained in this letter does not constitute a contract.

Don Robinson's optimistic letter to Peter Duncan.

Chapter One

September 1965 - Something's In the Air

Scarborough entrepreneur Don Robinson had an idea. This wasn't unusual - his life was one long list of ideas successfully transferred into reality. On this occasion Don had been listening to the original UK offshore station, Radio Caroline.

Since Easter 1964 this pioneering station had broken the monopoly of the BBC by broadcasting to the UK from a ship moored three miles off Clacton on the Essex coast. Within a few weeks Caroline had been joined by Radio Atlanta and shortly afterwards these two stations merged and the original Caroline ship sailed around Britain, broadcasting as she went, before mooring three miles off Ramsey in the Isle of Man.

The sea around Caroline South didn't stay quiet for long. A number of former military forts were seized by smaller radio operators and then just before Christmas 1965 the most successful radio station of all anchored just a mile away from

Caroline. This was Radio London, a slick American backed operation that employed highly experienced broadcasting staff and ran the hugely popular Top 40 music format.

Further north Radio Scotland also went on air from New Year's Eve 1965. Each part of Britain was being offered its own station. Finally the big conurbations of North East England were to have their broadcasting station when Don Robinson started planning Radio 270.

Don's working world was one of sensing a new opportunity ahead of the crowd. He registered his first company in 1961 and it gives a broad description of his enterprise.
Robinson's Promotions Ltd. was set up to "carry on the business of promoters of race meeting, sports matches, shows, exhibitions and competitions of all kinds".
Don also promoted bands at venues throughout Yorkshire and the North East. During a recording session with a young pop group he mentioned to the sound engineer an interest in starting an offshore radio station. The engineer, Peter Duncan, was employed by Tyne Tees Television and often helped Don on a freelance basis. Peter was immediately enthusiastic about the plan and used his contacts within the TV business to make initial enquiries about studio and transmission equipment.

At the same time Don contacted another friend, Bill Pashby, well known in Scarborough as a very experienced fisherman, who knew the unpredictable coastal waters and was well aware of the likely conditions once broadcasting had commenced.

Scarborough has many connections with Holland and it was through these contacts that Bill found a suitable boat for the enterprise in Scheveningen, just outside The Hague. At this time the original plan was to pre-record Radio 2 and Radio 4 type programmes on tape and send them out to the ship for transmission. A small boat was therefore quite suitable for a studio that would only contain a couple of tape machines and a sound mixer panel capable of allowing the occasional announcement to be made. However as the project progressed and became more sophisticated and the original ideas expanded, the limitations of a small boat were to haunt the enterprise throughout its short but eventful life.

The boat that Bill Pashby found in Holland was an old Dutch Lugger built in 1939. The type of fishing it was suitable for was superseded and it was no longer of any use to the trawling industry. The Oceaan 7 itself had a colourful past - during the war she was requisitioned by the German army for personnel transport along the Rhine. After the war the ship's seine netting days were over and she languished in port for many years before Bill Pashby made her owners a reasonable offer of £2,500.

The original conversation between Don Robinson and Peter Duncan took place in September 1965, some eighteen months after the arrival of Radio Caroline. Both the stations - Caroline North and South - were attracting huge pop audiences eager to escape from the dull programmes of the BBC - little changed since the launch of the Light Programme in 1945. The daily BBC diet included Housewives Choice, Music While You Work and Family Favourites - all designed to keep an elite band of musicians in clover. Cover versions by live orchestras interspersed with jolly banter between the bandleader and the compere offered nothing to the teenage record buyer of the mid sixties.

The only station catering for this new audience before Caroline was Radio Luxembourg. But the major record companies like EMI and Decca dominated the transmissions. Their sponsored programmes, while playing some Merseybeat and Motown, also had to include a broad spectrum of releases. Audiences had to compromise. A thirty-second snatch of the Beatles could be followed by the latest offering from Matt Monro.

The ship borne stations in their early days also broadcast a surprisingly wide selection of music, but in a more discriminating way. The best of British beat was mixed with classic stateside songs. Words like, hip, stylish and cool were regularly used to describe the output of Radio Caroline.

All through the fifties the BBC had tried to ignore the burgeoning rock and roll boom. At best they played insipid cover versions by the latest British youngsters signed up by powerful new pop managers.

The musicians and record companies had a very tight grip on the amount of records broadcast. The BBC was obliged to employ hundreds of musicians for "session" tapes and the record giants only allowed a limited amount of records played - this was called "needletime". Even when a disc was broadcast the cost was colossal. Today each record played on Radio One or Two costs the BBC about £100 in royalties. Local BBC stations also pay a proportionate fee for their music.

Operating outside the law, the offshore stations weren't caught up in these restrictions and could also disregard these music royalty charges.

Don Robinson the entrepreneur had clearly spotted an interesting new money-making machine for his business portfolio.

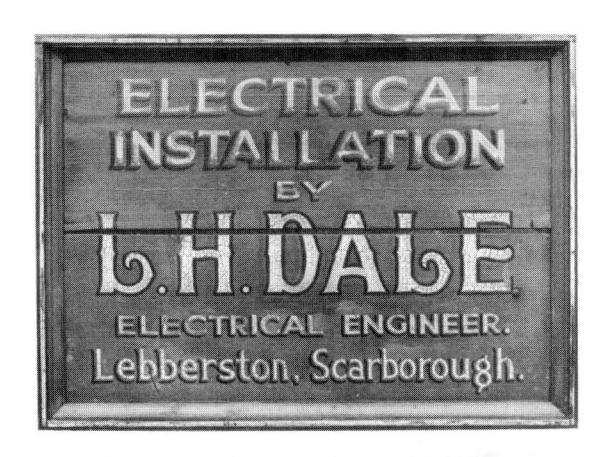

Chapter Two

Chasing the Dream - The Key Players

Radio 270 was synonymous with just three personalities - each bringing a wealth of wide and differing experience to the project. Smaller shareholders were later invited to contribute as switch-on time approached. The three major players were all strong, confident, self-made men. The interplay between them will be of great interest to students of business studies. How Don Robinson, Wilf Proudfoot and Leonard Dale dealt with the pressures of working together is a fascinating strand running through this inside account of Radio 270.

Don Robinson
Managing Director

"As a schoolboy I was hopeless. I could just about add up. My main interest at school was sport but I was also fascinated by entertainment and what made it happen" - From an interview in the "World's Fair" newspaper.

After his National Service, Don Robinson became a physical instructor at Scarborough College. In his spare time he took up amateur boxing and also played Rugby League for Hull KR. His first short-lived business enterprise was delivering fish to country areas ,"but handling cold, wet cod in the winter months was a bit grim". In the late fifties Don began promoting go-kart racing at venues all over the north. He was also involved in the opening of Scarborough's Candlelight Club. His sporting activity took him into the wrestling ring where he became the Empire light-heavyweight champion.

Greyhound racing was the next project during which time he consolidated all his interests into one company, Robinson Promotions, with his wife Jean as co-director. Wrestling matches became hugely popular and Don was the first promoter to have his shows broadcast on television. His daytime activities during the summer months were spent on Scarborough beach where he had a trampoline concession. He later became a director of the Flamingoland Zoo at Kirby Misperton.

Pop music was another money-spinner for him. He promoted shows at the Spa in Bridlington and at venues as far away as Leeds and Newcastle. One spectacular show at the Spa showcased the Applejacks and Gene Vincent - another sell-out all nighter at the Queen's Hall in Leeds starred the Small Faces and the Who. In 1965 Don also ventured into the recording business. Of three discs released by February 1966, one by Jimmy Echo, "After Tonight" sold 30,000 copies.

It was during this and other recordings that he first met Peter Duncan, a sound engineer at Tyne-Tees Television in Newcastle. During a recording session in the summer of 1965 Don asked Peter's advice about setting up an offshore radio station.

Leonard Dale
Chairman

"It is not eminent talent that ensures success, so much as purpose. The path of success in business is usually the path of common sense. In business, practice wisely and diligently improve." - from "Self-Help" published by Samuel Smiles in 1859 - one of Leonard Dale's guiding influences.

From small beginnings in the mid thirties, Leonard Dale built up the multi-million pound business, Dale Electric Ltd, a com-

Chasing the Dream - The Key Players

pany that has won the Queen's Award for export on more than one occasion.

His father owned a six-acre farm at Gristhorpe and when the family expanded he took over the larger Grange Farm at Lebberston. On the farm Leonard learnt all about the practicalities of running a business. He soon realised that an owner, for economic reasons, has to tackle problems often beyond his capabilities- "practice and improve". As a child, Leonard was enthralled by the mechanical world. His favourite was the box of Meccano.

After leaving school at age 14 in 1930 he put his back into helping on the farm. To earn some extra money he started making and selling chicken huts to neighbouring farms. A new development then came to the coast, electricity. When his father contracted a West Riding firm to install the necessary cables, Leonard took a keen interest and quickly learnt the basics. The local landlord was also an electrician and agreed to take Leonard on for just a few half days each week. Electricity then took over his life. He studied, learnt and applied this knowledge. One job in 1938 led to even more experience. He was asked to install emergency lighting and additional wiring at the new Brig Cinema in Filey. He told the manager that he was shortly to be married and enquired about any further work. He became assistant projectionist at the rate of 17s 6d for nine shows over each week. Within three weeks he was promoted to chief projectionist and his first film on that night was "South Riding" written by Winifred Holtby whose farmhouse in nearby Rudston he was later to rewire.

After the war he manufactured water pumps, electric welders and generating sets and by the mid fifties was handling orders for his reliable equipment from all over the world.

A Marine Generating Set Division was set up in 1965, headed by Leonard's second son, Gerald. And it was into Gerald's office that Peter Duncan was ushered one morning in early 1966 to enquire about a 60 kilowatts diesel generator. When questioned about the request, Peter felt unable to divulge further details, but that night when Gerald told his father about the meeting, it was decided to invite all the members of the consortium to the Gristhorpe factory. Here Leonard Dale was determined to find out more about the project. He wanted to know all about the transmitter and the auxiliary power needed for lighting, heating, and cooking.

Although the group displayed tremendous enthusiasm there seemed to be no clear idea of the scale of the project. Leonard and Gerald then left the room, suggesting they all had a few minutes to themselves to organise their thoughts. On returning, the group then asked Leonard if he would be prepared to accept the position of chairman of the new company, Radio 270. He said yes on the understanding that the radio company was to be completely legal and everything connected to the ship would have to comply with all the strict marine regulations.

A new and rather unusual project now settled on Leonard Dale's desk. A project that over the coming months was to prove rather uncomfortable for the chairman of such a prestigious company as Dale Electrics.

Wilf Proudfoot
Company Secretary - later Managing Director.

A new approach to the nation's problems -

"Each family would own an independent capital holding in industry - each family would enjoy a greatly enhanced standard of living and would at the same time have a profound political freedom, for the political power wielded by holders of public

Chasing the Dream - The Key Players

office will have been separated from economic power held by the citizens".

From "The Two Factor Nation - Or How to make the people Rich", written and published by Wilf Proudfoot and Rodney Shakespeare in 1977.

Politics and retail have been Wilf Proudfoot's abiding lifetime passions. At the age of 10 he returned from school to tell his father "I am going to be an M.P. some day".

He was born in the heart of the Durham coalfield at Crook and came to Scarborough to attend College from the age of 14. His first work experience was in the office of a Durham accountancy firm. In 1940 he was called up for war service and in the R.A.F. he became a technical training officer. His final two service years were spent in India and during his leave periods he travelled in the Himalayas. He described a prayer meeting held by Gandhi as one of the most moving experiences of his early life.

His family moved to Scarborough during the war after his father took over a grocery shop in Falsgrave Road. In 1946 Sergeant Wilf Proudfoot was released from the R.A.F. and with his gratuity bought his first grocery shop in Seamer - a familiar sight to the thousands of West Yorkshire holidaymakers streaming by car into Scarborough. This he soon expanded by including a newsagency for the village. In November 1954 he pioneered a self-service grocery store on the Eastfield estate.

Parallel with his business interests was his passion for politics. By 1947 he was a member of the Scarborough Young Conservatives and two years later was a candidate in the Seamer election which he lost by just 21 votes. Success came in 1950 when, at the age of 28, he won the Central Ward by-election - a position he held for five years.

He finally achieved his ambition when he was elected M.P.

for Cleveland and Whitby from 1959 to 1964. In the Commons he was known as "Decimal" Proudfoot because of his enthusiasm for the new currency.

For the next few years his political ambitions were to take a back seat when a new and exciting business venture appeared on the Scarborough marine horizon.

The Pirate Ship arrives for fitting out.

Chapter Three

Late 1965 - My Ship Is Coming In

The first announcement in the press was dated 25th September 1965. Don Robinson explained that Radio Yorkshire would beam pop music, commercials, weather reports and news flashes to a 120-mile radius of the north including Nottingham, Sheffield, Doncaster, York, Darlington and Newcastle - a potential audience of 10 million. A crew of nine would be aboard the ship and she would be anchored off Bridlington Bay. Don was aware that Radio Scotland would launch very shortly and that would be Britain's fifth offshore station. Radio Yorkshire would be the sixth and could commence within four months, but not before a name change. A Leeds based company objected saying they had already registered the name Radio Yorkshire in the 1950's.

Thus the frequency of 270 became incorporated into the new name and was chosen by Peter Duncan. He had scanned the international list of radio broadcasting wavelengths and spotted a possible gap in the medium wave. To avoid interference with overseas stations he looked at the location and power of transmitters near as possible to the centre of the medium wave band.

What he found across the whole of Europe on 1115 kHz (269 metres) were just a few local stations in Italy, Spain and Russia - all on relatively low power - non of which would be likely to interfere or be troubled by Radio 270.

Because of the severe weather conditions likely to be encountered on the North Sea, a plan was formulated to record programmes in a studio on-shore and then replay them from the ship. In January 1966 a studio was built in Newcastle where auditions were to be held for the radio presenters. A number of Tyne Tees Television personnel were asked to help out on a freelance basis. Among these were Head of Light Entertainment Len Marten and sound engineer Phil Sellman.

From these studios above Lindsey's Sea Food Restaurant in Neville Street, opposite the Central Station, commercials were made, street interviews were edited and short factual and Down Your Way type programmes were stockpiled. The main interviewers were Paul Burnett and Norman Wingrove.

As early as October 1965 Peter Duncan, later the station's technical director, received an optimistic letter from Don Robinson with details of the new boat. Bill Pashby had located the Oceaan 7 in Holland and Peter was asked to fly over to view it and suggest alterations for conversion to a radio ship. Don also revealed he was in touch with an American to take the position of Programme Controller.

A COMMERCIAL RADIO STATION for North East Coast

"Radio Yorkshire", as the Station will be called, has the transmitting equipment and operating frequency to beam programmes of "pop" music, weather reports, news flashes, etc., up to a distance of 120 miles. This will give coverage to most of the North Eastern area and the North Midlands including Newcastle, Leeds, Bradford, Sheffield, Nottingham, Leicester, the West Riding and the North East coast. It will start operating early in 1966.

"RADIO YORKSHIRE"
c/o BOX S98, HESLOCK LTD.,
Albemarle Chambers,
Albemarle Crescent, Scarborough

Also in October 1965 an advertising agent was appointed to handle the commercials side of the business. Heslock Ltd.

Shortly after the first announcement of the station's formation, Wilf Proudfoot approached Don Robinson expressing a desire to buy an advertising campaign for his supermarket chain. Within an hour or so, Don Robinson had personally gone round to speak to Wilf and invite him in as a shareholder. Sixty friends and business colleagues of the supermarket boss were then invited to a meeting at the Pavilion Hotel where more detailed plans were given. Wilf Proudfoot told the meeting that the project was high risk and they might as well stand on the Castle headland and throw their pound

Late 1965 - My Ship Is Coming In

notes into the wind! In spite of this warning, a total of £52,000 was raised from the new shareholders.

Back in Holland work began on refurbishing the Oceaan 7 which had not been in use for a decade. It was at this point that costs began to increase alarmingly. A Dutch engineering company had given a quote for repairs to the engine but when their bill was presented the price had doubled to £11,000 - the reason, they had sensed the urgency and the perceived wealth of an offshore radio station. A furious Leonard Dale went to Holland to sue the company but was told that the case would take a year to reach the Dutch courts. In the meantime the boat would stay moored in Holland. The inflated cheque was handed over.

The radio transmission system was originally to be a simple "T" type aerial - essentially a taut wire running along the length of the boat. This is the simplest method but has the disadvantage of a fluctuating signal depending on which direction the boat is pointing. For the best signal the ship has to be parallel to the coast. Once it drifts away from this position the signal on land is seriously impaired and the transmission distance greatly reduced. During January 1966 the plan was changed to incorporate a vertical lattice aerial - vastly increasing the costs - but also considerably increasing the transmission area.

The 137ft boat completed its expensive engineering overhaul in Holland and was passed as 100% seaworthy. Bill Pashby, the company's maritime director, then planned to sail for Scarborough but was delayed for three days by rough weather. The boat was finally sighted by the Scarborough lighthouse at 5.30am on Saturday 26th February 1966 and sailed in proudly on the morning tide, berthing at the Inner Harbour alongside the Vincent Pier. The yellow and black coloured ship arrived with an already over painted identification name - changed from the Dutch "Oceaan VII" to the anglicised "Ocean 7". Meeting her at the quayside was the lighthouse keeper, a customs official and members of the 270 board.

Two weeks were allocated for renovations as the interior was stripped to accommodate the radio equipment and also the living and sleeping quarters for the on-board crew. Twelve joiners were signed up to work in shifts over the full 24 hours a day for a fortnight. The work included new cabins, showers, a kitchen with refrigeration units to store up to 7cwt of meat, and generators, and a desalination unit to provide 200 gallons of fresh drinking water each day. A team of 30 electricians, plumbers and engineers, including Arthur Harding and Gordon MacIntyre from Leonard Dale's factory in Gristhorpe, also descended on the ship within hours of its arrival.

Wilf Proudfoot, now identified as joint managing director and secretary, explained the pressure on Ellambar Investments, the company behind the enterprise, "We are working to a deadline and there is not a minute to be lost. The ship must be fitted out in a fortnight if we are to start transmitting on time". Also visiting the harbour that Saturday morning were Don Robinson, the entertainments director and Leonard Dale, the Managing Director, who was to oversee the installation of his two Dale Electric generators.

The broadcast studios and living quarters for DJs and technicians were to be built in the old ice-room and fish hold. The ship's crew were to use the existing sleeping quarters in the bow. Once renovations were complete the ship was to sail for an unspecified destination for the fitting of the final piece of the jigsaw, the 162ft high aluminium transmitting mast - installation here would be deemed illegal. Once this work was complete the radio ship would arrive back off the Yorkshire coast to commence daily broadcasting from 7am to midnight. Within the estimated 120 mile radius of the transmitter lived a potential of fifteen million listeners. April 1st was to be the opening day of the north's very own Radio 270. But long before then the original directors, Don Robinson, Peter Duncan and Bill Pashby all felt unease about the enterprise.

Chapter Four

The Countdown to On-Air 1966

The prelude to the opening was to prove a difficult time for the company. Many people on the Yorkshire coast were not wholly convinced of the need for this new radio service. Even though the editor of the Scarborough Evening News was a shareholder in 270, a number of critical letters began to appear in the newspaper.

The first on Wednesday 16th March was from Mr D. H. Johnson of 53 West Avenue, Filey. He had expected many such letters but as non had appeared so far he felt he must point out that the transmitting frequency of 270 was likely to cause serious interference with the 261metres of the BBC Home Service. He pointed out that pop fans could hear their music on Radios Luxembourg, Caroline, London and a host of powerful continental stations, "as well as in countless milk bars and pubs nearby". Leonard Dale answered this by saying that the frequency had been chosen by an electronics expert and was similar to a number of stations in Italy. The power of Radio 270 would be fairly modest and could not interfere with the Italian broadcasts. He also added rather provocatively, "If the Home Service was overpowered by 270 it meant that the BBC needed a more powerful transmitter".

The criticism was not to stop there. Two days later another letter writer also opposed the station and suggested that the previous writer "might like to form a company to jam pirate radio broadcasts".

Radio 270 was clearly under siege and on Monday 21st March Leonard Dale, now described as Chairman and Joint

RADIO 270

Managing Director of Ellambar Investments Ltd, sought to put the record straight. He wanted to explain that far from just pop music, the new station would also offer daily talks from a vicar, three medical talks by a doctor and twice weekly gardening spots. There would be hourly news bulletins and each evening the station would offer a half-hour educational programme. He also then explained the allocation of radio frequencies throughout Europe. Of the 554 stations, 229 are officially authorised leaving some 325 outside the agreement. Radio Luxembourg for instance was never sanctioned to broadcast at a power of over a thousand kilowatts - 270 will use only a fraction of that - a mere 10kw. He also pointed out that Britain had no laws to make his company's broadcasts illegal. His company was properly set up following advice from Lloyd's of London. The copyright charge for the broadcasting of records on Radio 270 would be paid to the Performing Right Society.

To make the operation completely legal, the Scarborough based company, Ellambar Investments had loaned its £50,000 capital to two Panamanian companies registered in Puerto Cortes, Honduras. One company, Progresiva Compania Comercial S.A., owned the equipment and Maramado Cia, Naviera S.A. owned the boat. The agent for these companies in the UK was non other than 270 Programme Director and DJ, Noel Miller.

As well as fighting on the public relations front the owners also had to contend with technical difficulties which were increasing the pressure for a Friday April 1st launch.

Although the fitting of the mast was completed on time in Guernsey, the subsequent gales had forced the crew to begin tightening the rigging - something strongly advised against by the installer, Harry Spencer.

The installation of the transmitter was also delayed. Wilf Proudfoot was at this time in the middle of fighting the

Cleveland seat for the Conservatives but still found time to explain the problem. "We paid RCA in America £7,000 for the half-ton 10kw transmitter, but when it arrived on 22nd March last week, some parts were missing. These are now being flown in from New Jersey."

On Wednesday 30th March, the Oceaan 7 left Guernsey under tow from the fishing boat, "Courage". It was estimated the ship would arrive off Scarborough by 5am Friday, in time for the midday switch-on. During her journey up the East Coast music was apparently broadcast from the ship at half-power.

For Wilf Proudfoot this was an exhilarating time as business and politics mixed. He was the Conservative candidate for the Cleveland seat in the General Election. His political ambitions began as early as 1951 when he contested Hemsworth but lost to Labour. By 1955 he had made inroads into the Labour majority at Cleveland and only lost on a recount. In 1959 he was victorious at Cleveland when he overturned the opposition by a 1655 majority. However in the 1964 election this was reversed and he lost by a 4472 majority. In 1966 on the eve of 270's launch the Cleveland voters delivered a blow to him when they voted in Labour with a massive 11,880 majority.

Back with the radio business new broadcasting staff were revealed. The station was to have a radio vicar. The Reverend Hedley Pickard, the newly installed Vicar of Bempton, had thirteen years experience as a journalist before entering Lincoln Theological College in 1961. During his time on a newspaper in Bradford he regularly broadcast football commentaries for the BBC. Once Radio 270 was on air Mr. Pickard could have a potential congregation of 18 million.

Also joining the station was another experienced journalist, 38 year old York man, Stacey Brewer, also BBC trained, who had previously been heard on the Today programme and on Voice of the North. In recent years he had also been an inter-

RADIO 270

viewer on Tyne Tees Television. His new show on 270 would go out every weekday at 7pm when he'd be playing songs from his personal collection of 10,000 records. Luckily for Stacey he wouldn't even have to brave the ocean - his show would be pre-recorded in the comfort and warmth of the Newcastle studios. Another recruit was Ben Toney, previously the Programme Controller at the most successful of all the pirate stations, Radio London. Ben was taken on for a short time as a consultant as well as an on-air presenter.

Around this time, on the 4th March, the BBC issued a document outlining their plans for a pilot scheme of nine local radio stations. In typical BBC terms they described the programme output as "not being amplified jukeboxes of the kind familiar to people who have travelled overseas."

Radio 270's youngest DJ was signed up in mid-March. 17 year old Andy Kirk came from Collingham near Wetherby. A year before he was a pupil at Foxwood Secondary School in north Leeds and had been mesmerised by the flotilla of radio ships broadcasting to the UK. He decided to learn his trade at a hospital radio station in Leeds from May 1965. During these sessions he had interviewed Sandie Shaw and Unit Four Plus Two.

In October 1965 spotting an advert for new DJs on Radio Yorkshire he sent in a mock-up show and was given two interviews at the Newcastle studios. Once offered a position he resigned his trainee manager's job at his father's electrical firm to start this new maritime adventure. When asked about the future he replied, "I can see commercial radio growing fantastically in Britain during the next few years whether the Government allows it or not."

The countdown to the first 270 broadcast was rapidly approaching. Frantic phone calls were made to trace the missing transmitter equipment, but the Friday 1st April launch was set in stone. The boat moved into position on Thursday evening, all ready to broadcast from Friday at midday. In the record library were

The Countdown To On-Air 1966

songs from the latest Scarborough Top 10.

1. The Walker Brothers - The Sun Ain't Gonna Shine No More.
2. The Kinks - Dedicated Follower of Fashion.
3. Bob Lind - Butterfly.
4. Dave Dee, Dozy, Beaky, Mick and Tich - Hold Tight.
5. The Who - Substitute.
6. Spencer Davis Group - Somebody Help Me.
7. The Hollies - I Can't Let Go.
8. Val Doonican - Butterfly.
9. Crispian St. Peters - Pied Piper.
10. Cilla Black - Alfie.

press release   RADIO-270

WESTMINSTER BANK CHAMBERS
ST. NICHOLAS STREET, SCARBOROUGH, YORKSHIRE
TELEPHONES SCARBOROUGH 63541/2
TELEGRAMS TOSEVENO SCARBOROUGH
YOUR REF: OUR REF:

COMMERCIAL RADIO FOR THE NORTH EAST, YORKSHIRE AND MIDLANDS

MONDAY TO FRIDAY

Time			Programme	DJs
7.00 a.m.	–	9.00 a.m.	EARLY BIRD	(Ives/Kirk)
9.00 a.m.	–	11.00 a.m.	LEN MARTEN	(–)
11.00 a.m.	–	2.00 p.m.	LUNCHDATE	(Gale/Dewing)
2.00 p.m.	–	4.00 p.m.	SIESTA	(Wingrove/Burnett)
4.00 p.m.	–	6.00 p.m.	TEENBEAT 66	(Ives/Kirk)
6.00 p.m.	–	6.30 p.m.	STACEY BREWER SHOW	
6.30 p.m.	–	7.00 p.m.	THE WORLD TOMORROW	
7.00 p.m.	–	8.00 p.m.	LEN MARTEN SHOW	
8.00 p.m.	–	9.00 p.m.	AGENT 270	
9.00 p.m.	–	12.00 a.m.	PAUL BURNETT SHOW	(Wingrove/Burnett)

270270270270270270270270270270270270270270270270270270270702

Don Robinson's initial broadcasting schedule showing the two on-air teams of DJs

RADIO 270

In the Programme Policy memo sent to all presenters from Don Robinson were these important points.
Out of the news - a Top 10 song.
In each half hour another Top 10 tune, one golden oldie, one LP track, two American discs and two further tracks from the UK Top 40.
No song to be repeated in a three hour show. A maximum of four letters to be read out per hour.
Jingles left to the DJs discretion but should not be overdone.
References to bad weather and sea-sickness are to be avoided at all times.
References to the ship Ocean 270 are encouraged as are comments towards fishermen and happy holiday makers.

Slogans to be used frequently -
Radio 270- the young idea.
Your swinging boat on the North East Coast.
Radio 270-the station with a smile.
Get with the In-Set from the Outset on Radio 270.

The Closedown announcement - "The time is now midnight and that brings us to the end of another days broadcasting from Ocean 270. We shall be on the air again at 7am and we hope you will join us then. And now on behalf of the Captain, Crew and all the boys on board Ocean 270, this is........wishing you all a very, very good night. Goodnight."
Followed by the National Anthem

Working through the night on the 31st March engineers made modifications to the transmitter to circumvent the lack of essential spare parts. By Friday morning they knew that it was a futile effort. Just three vital condensers were missing and all attempts to tease the transmitter into activity had failed.

The Countdown To On-Air 1966

Back at the Grand Hotel the directors were anxiously awaiting the first announcement planned to be broadcast at one minute to midday. This was to be a prayer for all at sea and a blessing for the ship recorded by the radio vicar, Hedley Pickard. But whenever the directors frantically retuned their transistors all they heard around 270 was a faint signal from the southern based pop pirate Radio London. Four miles offshore surrounded by thick mist was a silent 270.

One of the largest shareholders, Tom Stephenson, managing director of Scarborough coach builders, Plaxtons tried to explain the difficulties but it was left to Don Robinson to give a detailed breakdown of the problems. "We had intended to start broadcasts today but are still short of a couple of condensers for the transmitter. They only cost a few pounds each but without them we're unable to send out full strength signals".

The 14 man team on board the ship was understandably frustrated and tried their best to fight off the effects of a strengthening north-easterly. But worse was to come.

The DJ staff on the Oceaan 7 included programme director Roger Gale (23), Paul Burnett (23), Andy Kirk (18), Allen Ives (18) and Bob Dewing (36). The station's technical director Peter Duncan was also on board during the worst gales in living memory. As the wind speed and the height of the waves increased hourly, the staff knew that Friday night's weather conditions wouldn't improve.

Because of the ferocious sea, the Dutch crew had become so concerned about the swaying mast that they had tightened the stay ropes. By Saturday morning the gale showed no sign of abating and the stays were now at their most taut. Disaster was imminent. One of the ropes snapped creating massive tension on the others. The light aluminium mast snapped and lurched over the side. There was no other sensible solution but to abandon it. Peter Duncan set the crew to with axes to cut the ropes

RADIO 270

and ditch the mast before it created instability for the ship.

Just after 9am on Saturday 2nd April the £10,000 mast joined Davy Jones's locker four miles off the coast. To compound the despair, at that same time, a small fishing boat set sail from Scarborough with the missing transmitter components which had arrived in London from New Jersey on Friday night and had been sent up overnight by car. An insurance claim to Lloyd's for the abandoned mast was refused because safety advice had gone unheeded. A new "Sparlight" mast had to be purchased by the company at a cost of £2,000.

Not only was the prospect of broadcasting fading away, there was also the matter of a well-stocked kitchen to think about. Just before the ship had left Scarborough she had been loaded up with supplies including 1000 sausages, 500 rashers of bacon, 150 loaves of bread, 100lb of cheese, six legs of roast lamb, 100 pairs of kippers, turkeys, fish and a ton of potatoes.

The disaster was about to become even worse. A decision was made to sail the ship back to the safety of Scarborough harbour, but when the motor started a cable from the mast became entangled in the propeller. A distress signal was sent out and two local keel boats started to make their way out but this was quickly cancelled after the cable was freed by cutting away more of the mast section. Amazingly the mast lay at the bottom of the ocean for twenty-three years before being rediscovered.

The ship arrived back in port to be greeted by a dismayed group of directors. Many questions needed to be answered not least of which was how quickly this public relations disaster could be rectified. The aerial mast had been erected in Guernsey and a representative was summoned up to the ship.

The Countdown To On-Air 1966

Saturday 2nd April The Ocean 7 back in harbour minus the mast.

Also within a few days more delay was introduced when the Board of Trade insisted that a British certificate of seaworthiness had to be produced. Although one had been obtained in Holland and was acceptable to Lloyd's, the Board of Trade insisted on a more detailed survey of the ship. This meant taking the boat to another port with better facilities. Grimsby was chosen and the Oceaan 7 set sail on the 19th April.

All this delay had created tremendous boardroom tensions and in a cost cutting exercise it was decided to close the Newcastle recording studio. Earlier, on the 12th April, Peter Duncan confirmed the rumours and stated that Wilf Proudfoot had taken the decision "off his own bat". The official reason given was the problem of communication between Newcastle and Scarborough but clearly a rift was

RADIO 270

appearing in the ranks as Don Robinson's original team felt they were being hijacked by the newer directors.

By mid April Leonard Dale was Joint Managing Director and Chairman, together with Wilf Proudfoot as Joint Managing Director and Secretary. Don Robinson was no longer Managing Director of Radio 270 but now Manager of Programmes. Others on the board were Peter Asquith, Hilton Armstrong, Roland Hill, Peter Duncan, Bill Pashby and Tony Rylands.

Band leader Cyril Stapleton was also a major shareholder. His musical offerings to the nation included the fifties hits, Blue Star, The Happy Whistler and Nick Nack Paddy Wack. In 1964 he wrote and produced "The Blue Beat", the first song for Chris Farlowe's early band, The Beazers. With his BBC Showband radio programme he also gave Matt Munro his first big break.

By January 1966 he had joined Pye Records as A & R director and released the single, March of the Diddymen. He also produced and masterminded the concept of the Max Bygraves Singalong albums. Because the record companies officially didn't approve of offshore radio, Cyril tactfully put his 270 shareholding in the name of his wife, who then took her place on the board of directors.

Whilst in Grimsby the question of ship registration was raised by Board of Trade officials. The papers that registered her in Panama had been lost and in all the build up to the launch this fact had slipped through the net. A new set had to be processed and to make sure there were no more delays, Wilf Proudfoot flew on the 13th May to South America with the new application forms. In the town of Tabusigalpa he encountered a classic case of non-cooperation unless the correct sweeteners were offered to officials. His visit to Panama also cost Wilf Proudfoot the local

The Countdown To On-Air 1966

election. He was to have been in town to fight the Falsgrave ward, but missed the vote and didn't return to Scarborough until the following week.

A debate was held by Scarborough Council on the question of whether it was ethical for them to advertise on the station. It was known that 70% of all visitors to Scarborough came from the potential transmission area of Radio 270. The Mayor-Elect, Councillor E J Pilgrim, being a shareholder, was clearly in favour, but others were vehemently against the proposal. However the scheme to book twelve 15 second spots at a cost of £200 was finally approved.

The proposed new launch date of Saturday 14th May was however lost as the ship was still in Grimsby.

In Scarborough on Friday 3rd June the new Scene One discotheque opened - and the following day Radio 270 returned to Scarborough - complete with official certificates and the all important new mast. Test transmissions signals on 1115 kilocycles commenced Tuesday the 7th and amateur radio hams reported a good signal. A letter sent by a listener at this time reported a weak signal in Leeds but the station replied that a full strength signal would be broadcast shortly.

And so on Saturday 11th June Radio 270 began official transmissions- although without any commercials. This was explained by the lack of power, the ship was transmitting at only quarter power and it was felt that in order to give customers a proper service, the adverts would be kept back until a full 10kw could be achieved. Even at reduced power listeners could hear the station in most parts of the north including Doncaster, Leeds and Grantham.

The Countdown To On-Air 1966

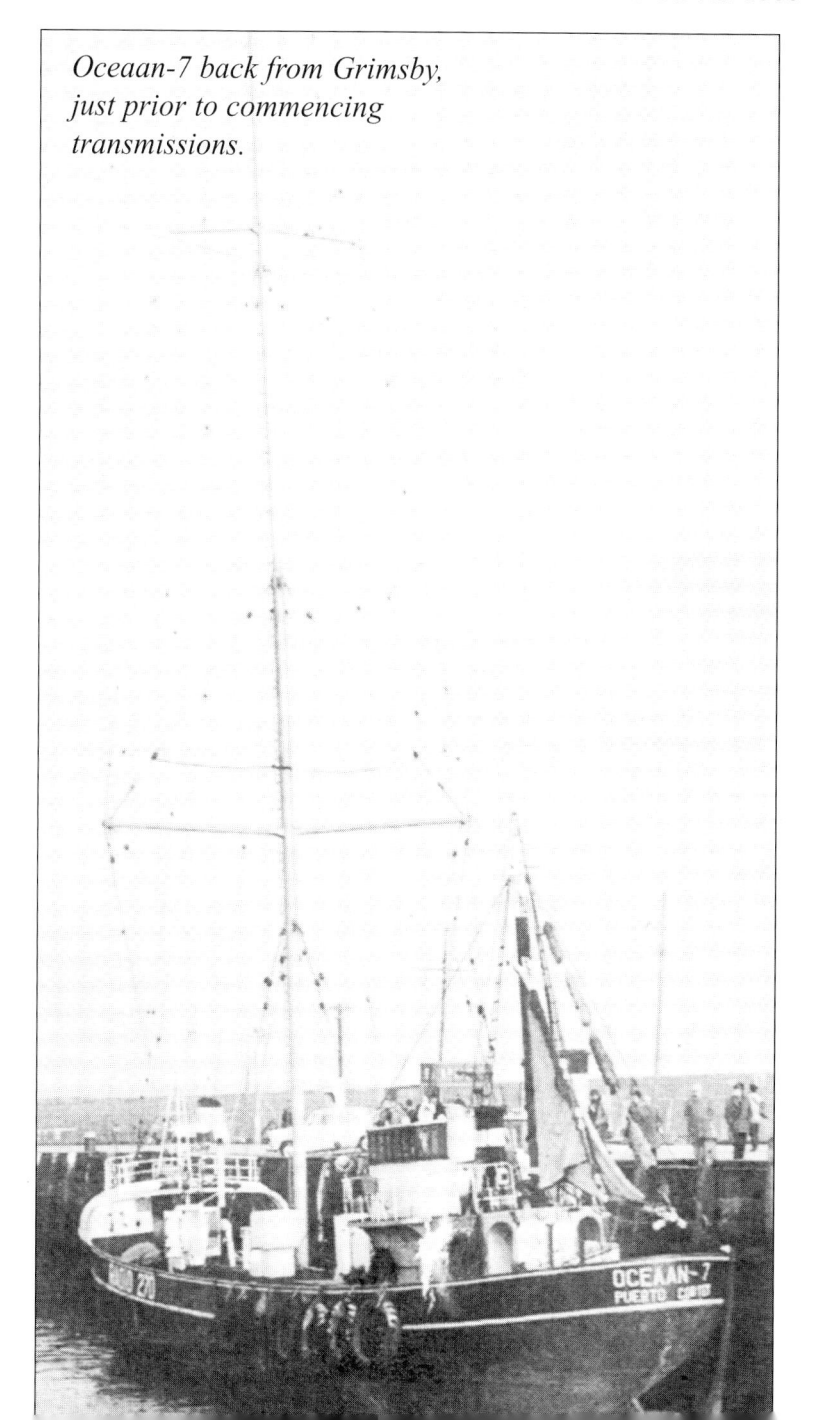

Oceaan-7 back from Grimsby, just prior to commencing transmissions.

RADIO 270

Chapter Five

Finally On- Air 1966

June 1966

Radio 270 Fun 40 - TOP FIVE

1. **Frank Sinatra- Strangers in the Night**
2. **The Rolling Stones - Paint It Black**
3. **The Troggs - Wild Thing**
4. **The Merseybeats - Sorrow**
5. **The Mamas and the Papas - Monday Monday**

A team of six DJ's and seven crew were on board for the launch. Wilf Proudfoot told the DJs they had to start with one of two songs, either the chart-topper at the time or the novelty tune, I Love Onions by girl singer, Laurie. The nation's number one song won - Strangers in the Night by Frank Sinatra. Roger Gale was the first DJ on air and just to illustrate the music variety listeners could expect the second record was the more up-tempo soul classic from Wilson Pickett, 634 - 5789. Laurie's chirpy song on Decca though became a firm favourite in those early weeks.

Also on board the radio ship for the opening broadcasts were Noel Miller, Dennis Straney, Pete Bowman, Paul Burnett and Andy Kirk. The other DJs, Allen Ives and Bob Dewing who had been there for the April launch had fallen by the wayside. During the two and a half months enforced silence, the DJs had been out selling airtime commercials - all for 15% commission.

RADIO 270

This was their only income. Andy Kirk recalls he wasn't paid at all during this period of seven weeks. Clearly a difficult time - the ability to be a DJ doesn't necessarily give you the skills to cold call on businesses to sell advertising. In spite of the difficulties, over £60,000 of advertising had been booked for the coming months.

> **TUCKLEY AND CO**
> 16 Pavilion Square
> Scarborough
> Telephone 3102
> AUCTIONEERS AND ESTATE AGENTS
>
> ## YOUR HOUSE ON THE AIR
>
> WE ARE ARRANGING A SERIES OF BROADCASTS ON RADIO 270 AS THE FIRST ESTATE AGENCY TO ADVERTISE TO THEIR FIFEEN MILLIONS LISTENING PUBLIC SPREAD OVER 200 MILES AROUND SCARBOROUGH.
>
> If you have property to sell, ring us today, and take advantage of our forward-looking approach to house sales.
>
> We believe there are many people wishing to live in Scarborough, and we are prepared to reach them and offer your property with every available means.
>
> More properties are required by our ever-increasing list of applicants. We require houses, bungalows, flats, businesses, hotels, shops and farms.
>
> 'PHONE TODAY: OUR ADVERTISING CAN BENEFIT YOU

A novel idea to sell houses by the company that eventually handled the sale of the Oceaan 7 ship.

Finally On-Air 1966

The DJ line up was chosen from some 600 applicants. However only Andy Kirk, from Collingham near Wetherby, had come via this route. The others were mostly experienced presenters.

Shareholder Cyril Stapleton, the band leader and personal friend of Wilf Proudfoot, had expressed disquiet about the way the station was being run and introduced Australian Noel Miller to the ship just before the June launch. Noel was the new Programme Director - effectively demoting Roger Gale who had been signed up in that position for the April launch. Roger was now named as Senior DJ.

Noel brought in another experienced Australian, Dennis the Menace. Roger Gale was previously Programme Controller at Radio Scotland. In June he was to meet up again with another Radio Scotland presenter, Pete Bowman, who had learnt his trade at the Top Rank in Newcastle. Paul Burnett from the Top Rank Dance Hall in Darlington, had gained his radio skills with the Aden Forces Broadcasting Service.

Each presenter was on board for two weeks, their third week was on land selling commercials at 15% commission, and their final week of the month was time off. Their wage packets weren't exactly bulging - at £25 per week, but this was certainly higher than many other small stations. And considering their only expenses through the month were for their week off, when they normally did personal appearances at local dance halls, it proved to be a very attractive way of life for adventurous young men.

The North Sea of course was one down side to this exciting existence. Even in the height of summer a gale can come along to worry even the most experienced

RADIO 270

crew.
Another concern is thick sea fog. On one day in June Paul Burnett recalled being petrified when the crew ran around in a state of panic banging metal bars to alert a massive oil tanker to the 270 mooring. "Suddenly out of the fog we saw this massive wall of steel !"
On the evening of 27th June, only a few weeks after going on-air, the station was again silenced when a safety device on the transmitter cut in after copper wire had short circuited on the mast. Wilf Proudfoot went to the ship on the keelboat "Courage" to assess the difficulties and it was decided to expedite repairs quickly by sailing the ship into Scarborough harbour where it arrived the next day just after noon. The lack of spare parts though kept the station off air until the first week in July.

July 1966

Radio 270 Fun 40 TOP FIVE

1. The Beatles - Paperback Writer
2. The Kinks - Sunny Afternoon
3. Ike and Tina Turner - River Deep Mountain High
4. Gene Pitney - Nobody Needs Your Love
5. Percy Sledge - When a Man loves a Woman
A friendly wave to the visitors on a Pleasure Boat

Finally On-Air 1966

On Wednesday 6th July a newspaper ad told listeners,

"LOUD AND CLEAR - Radio 270 is heard even in Turkey."

Also in the feature were these -

Two Diesel Electric Generating plants which provide the whole of the Electric power on the off shore Radio Station, Radio 270, supplied by Dale Electric, Filey.

Flamingo Park Zoo, Malton to Pickering Road.
Open every day. We wish Radio 270 the Best of Luck.

Retailers - listen to the Gifts Galore Show on Radio 270 - 3.30 to 4pm every Sunday with the "Deliberate Mistake Contest"
Exciting prizes to be won - Radiograms, 3 piece suites, Refrigerators, washing machines etc.
If you like it write to Gifts Galore, 21 Wade Lane, Leeds 2

All records heard on station 270 are available from Jeavons for Records, 35 Percy Street and 46 Pudding Chare, Newcastle.

RADIO 270 the NorthEast's first commercial radio.
Heard it yet?
It's not just a station, it's a sensation all over the north and midlands and even overseas. It's hit 'em in Holland like a hole in the sea wall!

And it's got something for everybody - Up to the minute news bulletins, weather reports, competitions and special offers.

RADIO 270

"Pops" too a Plenty - but not just for the kids. Teenagers may go for Nancy Sinatra, but other prefer her old man. All age groups catered for on 270.

Tune in now to the most wide awake entertainment ever to take to the air - supplied by Roger Gale, Dennis the Menace, Paul Burnett, Hal York, Neddy Noel and all.

And listen, these characters are all like crazy! No foolin' they're literally giving away LP's and other things like that all the time. So tune in now and enter the competitions while they're still getting away with it.

270 it's a Rave on Medium Wave!

Behind the scenes tensions were building up between the controllers. It was clear that policy differences were soon to come to a head. On 6th July Don Robinson announced he was leaving to form a new radio company. Don had quit as a 270 director, but kept his shareholding. At the same time Chief DJ Roger Gale also resigned citing policy differences and "too much interference by Wilf Proudfoot."

This was all against the background of proposed government action to close the radio ships and forts. On the same day as Don Robinson announced his departure, the Postmaster General, Anthony Wedgwood Benn, told parliament that legislation against the stations would be introduced before the summer recess. A cold wind of change was about to blow the ships off course and the mood quickly changed from buccaneering fun to a bleak future.

Don Robinson's new radio venture received very little publicity. It was all conducted under a veil of secrecy mindful of the

Finally On-Air 1966

government's anti-pirate stance.

Don knew of the problems caused by bad weather to Radio Caroline South. Their boat, the Mi Amigo, was beached during some ferocious gales and whilst repairs were undertaken in Holland another radio ship had been hired to beam out Caroline's programmes. The ship was the Cheeta II, formerly used for the Swedish pop station Radio Syd. Impending Swedish anti-pirate legislation and thick pack ice had forced her to cease broadcasting and she was offered for hire to the Caroline organisation. Once the Mi Amigo had been repaired Cheeta II relayed the new Caroline shows for a short time before taking anchor and awaiting new instructions from her owner.

In the meantime Don Robinson had once again spotted an opportunity. Here was a well-equipped radio ship available, thus avoiding huge start up costs. Don had seen the success of Radio Caroline North, now anchored off Ramsey in the Isle of Man. Obviously there would be no demand for a similar station but perhaps a less frenetic style might just appeal to an older audience. Don therefore teamed up with the easy listening station, Radio 390, which broadcast from an old fort in the Thames estuary. This was the deal. 390 agreed to pay £10,000 to purchase the VHF transmitter on Cheeta II for use on their fort.

Don's idea was to take their easy listening format and broadcast using a new Medium Wave transmitter from the Cheeta II off the Isle of Man as Radio 390 North. Peter Duncan was the front man to complete the purchase of the ship (for £30,000 to include the new MW transmitter) and plans were made to sail her to a Welsh port. Sadly the deal was caught up in the usual offshore maritime tangle. A cargo handling dispute at Kennedy airport meant a delay in the supply of the new transmitter and a penalty clause in the agreement meant that the Cheeta II owner soon owed Don Robinson £12,000. When the transmitter eventually arrived at Amsterdam airport it was found smashed to pieces. After a meeting it was agreed to void the whole deal before threatened court costs mounted. To add to the tension on 21st July a customs officer boarded the boat and nailed a writ to the mast after a towing company claimed salvage after helping when she broke anchor. A dispute followed about the true owner of the ship and the vessel remained under arrest in Harwich until November, by which time Don's dream of another station had evaporated.

The ship eventually was taken to the Gambia where she broadcast as Radio Syd before becoming a floating restaurant. Apparently she later sank but can still be seen in Bathurst Harbour.

On the North Sea off Scarborough, July was another eventful month for Radio 270. With the impending threat of legislation a public relations onslaught was needed to avoid a loss of worried advertisers.

Wilf Proudfoot laid out the positive aspects of having a station on the NE coast. Over 60% of the population had tuned in to hear the music and the DJ banter. Many local firms were using the medium and were reporting good responses to their adverts. Asked about the future he said, "I now believe more than ever that this medium must be free. Britain has a tradition of free speech and freedom of the press - and radio is just another medium by which this can be continued. We may eventually end up with a radio station for each town. Scarborough could support three stations and Middlesbrough could have as many as six."

"As far as 270 is concerned we shall go on working up to the very last day. The shutdown is unlikely to happen before next Easter and possibly much later - if it does indeed ever come at all".

Tourism boss, Steve Fewster, explained the publicity aspect of a Scarborough station. "We have had much more publicity on the

Finally On-Air 1966

radio than we could ever have bought. Its broadcast area contains up to 80% of our holidaymakers. We would certainly miss it if it had to go out of business".

Scarborough Town Council had just agreed to spend £200 on an advertising campaign in the next few weeks in the run up to the school holidays. Already eight million listeners heard the word Scarborough up to 120 times a day just from DJ mentions.

Other advertisers were also enthusiastic about the station. The removal firm, Speed of Barwick Street, Scarborough expressed approval of their campaigns, and Flamingo Park Zoo near Pickering (owned by Don Robinson) said their attendances had increased whilst across the country other zoos were in decline.

However back on board ship, things were not looking quite so rosy.

August 1966

Radio 270 Fun 40 - TOP FIVE

1. The Troggs - With a Girl Like You
2. Chris Farlowe - Out of Time
3. Los Bravos - Black is Black
4. Chris Montez - The More I See You
5. Georgie Fame - Get Away

RADIO 270

What should have been a perfect month on the calm summer sea with plenty of visitors sailing out to see the ship, had suddenly turned sour.

Five of the DJs quit the station over conditions on board.

The row had come to a head after the dismissal of top DJ "Dennis the Menace", 27 year old Australian Dennis Straney. The other DJs who mutinied were Pete Bowman, Alex Dee, Paul Burnett and Andy Kirk. This of course followed the resignation of Roger Gale just a few weeks before. Holding the station together for a short time were Noel Miller, the Programme Director, and Newsman Hal Yorke.

Hal Yorke in the compact 270 studio.

Finally On-Air 1966

The frustration aboard had led to some practical jokes. One, which led to Dennis the Menace's dismissal, was a vacuum cleaner stunt. Noel Miller was described by some on board as a "pompous ass....". For some light-hearted revenge the DJs filled the nozzle of a vacuum cleaner with flour. They then inserted the nozzle into the studio just in front of the DJ panel. As Noel Miller was about to start his show, the others switched on the cleaner in the blow position. Noel was covered from head to toe in the baking flour and was unable to clean himself for the duration of the three-hour show. When the DJs went to "investigate" the incident which Noel had mentioned on the air, Dennis the Menace issued the immortal line - "Noel, I didn't know you were into flour power."

However only a day after being sacked by Noel Miller, the company issued another statement saying that it had all been a misunderstanding and that Dennis the Menace, also the station's promotion manager, had been reinstated and was broadcasting as normal. "It has all been a storm in a teacup - not even a teacup" said Noel Miller, " we remain the best of friends".

Noel Miller's hand written Top 40.

RADIO 270

September 1966

Radio 270 Fun 40 - TOP FIVE

1. The Beatles - Yellow Submarine / Eleanor Rigby
2. The Beach Boys - God Only Knows
3. The Small Faces - All or Nothing
4. Napoleon XIV - They're Coming To Take Me Away - Ha, Haa
5. Dave Berry - Mama

An MP planned to visit the ship on a fact-finding mission, but was prevented from sailing by atrocious gales and storms. Paul Bryan, MP for Howden and the Opposition frontbench spokesman on broadcasting said he wanted to see as many stations as possible to acquaint himself with the proposed bill to suppress offshore broadcasters. He was in favour of commercial radio, "But at present we are in the ridiculous position where the only way is to put it out at sea."

Eventually on Tuesday 13th September, he clambered aboard the Oceaan 7 and afterwards said he was impressed by the operation. "Millions enjoyed the programmes and the Labour government ought to plan legal land-based stations before banning the pirates. These low powered stations could be a useful source of revenue for the Government and the present stations with all their experience should be able to run them." Later as he stepped back onto the harbour with his shoes and trousers wet through, he did comment "What a hell of a way to have to run a broadcasting station." His preference in music was opera and choral singing rather than beat music, he added, and he didn't envy the disc-jockeys one bit, "I dread to think what it will be like out there during the winter."

Finally On-Air 1966

DJ Paul Burnett certainly knew. He rather famously was sick on air whilst reading out a Proudfoot supermarket commercial for fried bacon.

Two days later Radio 270 had to move temporarily to more sheltered waters off Bridlington Bay after being rocked by yet more stormy seas.

October 1966

Radio 270 Fun 40 - TOP FIVE

1. Jim Reeves - Distant Drums
2. The Who - I'm A Boy
3. The Supremes - You Can't Hurry Love
4. Sonny and Cher - Little Man
5. Roy Orbison - Too Soon To Know

RADIO 270

Wilf Proudfoot proposed two novel programming ideas this month. He offered airtime to students from Sheffield University and he hoped they would use the station to produce stimulating and thought provoking programmes. "They can discuss anything they wish, even to knock pirate radio. Only bad language is banned." Sheffield and Durham Universities took up the offer - Newcastle expressed enthusiasm but never delivered a tape. Sadly of the few tapes received most were badly recorded and barely audible. Some material concentrated on sex and lurid humour. Listener reaction was nil and the idea of educated University students providing stimulating discussion programmes was soon dropped.

Another idea was to offer firms free adverts to recruit staff. The coverage of the station from Newcastle in the north down to Sheffield and Lincoln, and over to West Yorkshire should give unrivalled opportunities to reach out and find skilled workers. "We are doing this as a service to the community. We want to see the area thrive and want to do anything we can to help," added the station.

The power of radio to help in the community was exemplified this month when an appeal was made to find a missing 14-year-old girl who had run away from home. Marie Williams from Redcar heard the broadcast and returned home after a short stay with friends. Her mother and local police officers praised the station for their co-operation during the search.

A week later the station was rocked by the resignation of skipper Bill Pashby. He was said to be "sick of crewmen being sacked or leaving the vessel. I've quit the board because I have lost confidence in the managing director, Wilf Proudfoot. Too many good men are being sacked from the ship at the wrong time of year." The argument was precipitated by the board's decision to replace the Dutch skipper with an English one.

Bill Pashby was a founding member of the consortium that

formed the station a year earlier. His shareholding was £1000 but often at the board meeting he felt decisions had been voted on before his arrival. He added he felt there had been too much interference by Mr.Proudfoot.

Also in October Parliament heard about Maritime radio interference to lifeboats. Of 49 cases of wireless breakthrough the most recent was on the 2nd October between the Scarborough lifeboat and Radio 270. During a search for a yacht, the communications officer aboard the lifeboat stated that music had broken through on their channel and he had contemplated switching to the distress frequency. The problem was increased because the lifeboat passed very close to the station and almost any more powerful transmitter would have interfered. Previously relations between 270 and the lifeboats had been cordial, with the stations often broadcasting RNLI charity appeals. Wilf Proudfoot asked why the service had not contacted him personally to try to rectify the situation, " Other stations could have caused the problem - at the time there was continental interference to both BBC TV and Radio."

November 1966

Radio 270 Fun 40 - TOP FIVE

1. The Four Tops - Reach Out I'll Be There
2. The Hollies - Stop Stop Stop
3. The Troggs - I Can't Control Myself
4. New Vaudeville Band - Winchester Cathedral
5. Paul Jones - High Time

RADIO 270

a newspaper headline at the beginning of the month.

Pirate DJs fear coble 'taxi' may sink

7 NOV 1966

OUR SCARBOROUGH REPORTER

PIRATE radio disc jockeys' fears were dispelled over the weekend in an announcement from the company controlling the pirate radio ship Radio 270.

At a Scarborough meeting on Saturday, three of the nine disc jockeys, declared a vote of no confidence in the sea worthiness of a small boat which the company uses to ferry the DJs to and from the ship, three and a half miles off Scarborough. They held their meeting while the ship was in port awaiting engine repairs. Nearby was a 26ft., blue coble, built in Scarborough, the cause of their fear.

A DJ said after a stormy secret meeting: "We cannot divulge our names because we are scared of losing our jobs, but not as we are of having to that little boat to R...

The Mutineers Right: Andy Kirk Bottom Left: Alex Dee & Bottom Right: Leon Tippler

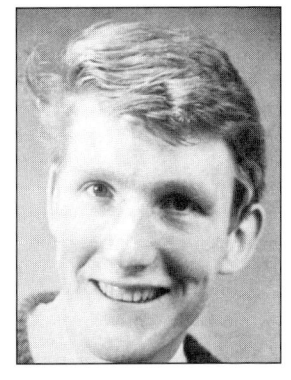

Finally On-Air 1966

DJs and crew held a secret meeting just before boarding the 26ft blue coble, the cause of their protest. Bill Pashby, who quit the board a few weeks earlier, commented "the boat is junk." Confirming this disquiet was Chief Engineer, Sean Webb. "I do not think this little boat is capable of safely running to and from the ship especially with the winter coming on. It's an old boat

and its engine is not at all it should be." Deck hand Gordon Vasey also commented, " If I am asked to go out on this little boat I shall refuse."
Sean Webb also revealed the pressures of life at sea. "The way the radio station is being run has already broken up my home life. I was out on the ship for five-and-a-half weeks and my wife Mary left me. It's about time we got a maritime director back on the board."
It was left to Chairman Leonard Dale to resolve the mutiny. "I knew the DJs didn't like the boat, but at this time of year it is impossible to charter a tender to get them out to the ship. In

future we intend to bring the ship near to the harbour when we finish transmitting and will pick them up there. We shall only use the coble when the weather is calm enough to ferry them to it."

On Wednesday 16th November the worst gale in living memory blew up. A 9-inch diameter mizzenmast jib was snapped in three places. The waves were so high that seawater washed over the side and penetrated electrical equipment. The three DJs on board gave up live broadcasts and were forced to resort to taped music. Deck hand D. Murphy added, "I have spent ten years in the Royal Navy and have been through storms in the tropics but I have never known anything like this. I have no intention of going back on board and am looking for a job elsewhere."

The three presenters on board, Andy Kirk, 19, Leon Tipler, 24, and Alex Dee, 20, issued an ultimatum to the company which was reported in the national press. At 7.30am on the Thursday morning the ship went off the air completely.

Said Andy Kirk: "The waves were gigantic - we thought the ship was going to capsize. We are not going back aboard that ship until we get some promises from the company. Either the ship is moved nearer the calmer Bridlington Bay or we are taken back to harbour as soon as a severe gale warning is issued."

Leonard Dale responded by saying decisions about whether to come inshore are entirely up to the captain. "He is very reliable and these DJs are exaggerating the danger."

Wilf Proudfoot added that if 270 was unsafe the company would abandon the project. Asked about the ultimatum he said, "I haven't seen these people - I haven't anything to do with the staff. The programme controller hires and fires deejays, and the captain hires and fires crew."

The next day all three DJs were fired. A furious Alex Dee told reporters that when they finally reached Bridlington there was

Finally On-Air 1966

no one to meet them and they had to search for a taxi to bring them back to Scarborough. "All the company seems to want to do is fill their own pockets with money at anyone else's expense. They don't care what kind of sound they put out as long as the money flows in. I am working as a guest DJ in Wetherby tonight because I had agreed to deputise for Andy before this afternoon's announcement that we had been fired." His 18-year-old girlfriend, jazz dancer Gillian Carroll said, "I heard what was happening on the radio and was absolutely terrified. I wept. I was sure I would never see Alex again."

....
Wetherby Town Hall
Friday 18th November 1966
7.45 - 11.45
Dance to the Sensational Sounds of Television, Radio and Recording Stars,
The Lollipop Band.
The Fabulous Radio 270 DJ Andy Kirk spins the discs.
Ready Steady Go-Go Dancer Jill Carroll.
Admission 7/6
Don't miss a really fabulous night with the Stars
....

Brenda Park, girlfriend of Andy Kirk, said, "I'm glad they gave him the sack. I was scared to death every time I knew he was at sea."
Andy added, "I was so keen to become another Jimmy Savile, I worked for the company for free for seven weeks. Noel Miller told me this on the telephone,
" We are terminating your employment because we cannot afford such bad publicity in the Press" - those were his exact words."

'Pirate' DJ: I'm glad they sacked him, says girl friend

Our Scarborough reporter.

A PIRATE radio disc jockey's girl friend said yesterday: "I'm glad they gave him the sack. I was scared to death everytime I knew he was at sea and heard him broadcast."

Andy Kirk, 19, one of the first disc jockeys to be employed by Radio 270 when it began broadcasts off Scarborough last June, was fired last Friday along with two other DJs following remarks they made to the Press.

The ship had been out in a gale, which forced the former Dutch fishing vessel to seek shelter in Bridlington Bay.

In a Press interview, the disc jockeys, Kirk, Alex Dee, 20, a Londoner and Leon Tipler, 24, of Kidderminster said that water had got into the studio and sparks had flashed around it.

They suggested that in future they would not work on the boat unless it was stationed near to Bridlington Bay or brought inshore when gales were imminent.

'Rubbish'

Andy Kirk who gave up a job in his father's electrical business in Leeds to become a pop sound disc jockey on the ship said: "The life appealed to me. I think I was the first applicant to be accepted as a DJ. I was so keen to become another Jimmy Savile that I worked for the company for seven weeks free.

"It has been rumoured that disc jockeys on Radio 270 must not talk to the Press. This is a load of rubbish. After we spoke to a national newspaper reporter and outlined our ideas for the future safety of the ship, we were sacked."

His girl friend, Brenda Park, a comptometer operator at Leeds University said: "Thank heavens they fired him. I was scared when I knew he was on board."

Andy Kirk added: "I was told on the telephone by the programme controller Noel Miller, who is also a disc jockey 'we are terminating your employment because we cannot afford such bad publicity in the Press'—those were his exact words."

Alex Dee said: "All the company who run this ship seem to do is to fill their own pockets at anybody's expense."

His girl friend, Gillian Carroll Jazz dancer, 18-year-old said: "When I heard on the radio what was happening out at sea during the gale that night, I was terrified."

Yesterday Radio 270 was still in Scarborough harbour, where she was said to be under-

Andy Kirk at the microphone.

Finally On-Air 1966

270 Programme Controller, Noel Miller, issued a statement.

"Three DJs were dismissed today for not obeying company policy in that they talked to the Press without informing the management. Their reports about the storm were exaggerated. I lay down a verbal rule with all the DJs they must not talk to the Press without discussing the matter with the company first. If DJs went to the Press every time something happened we would be annihilated sales-wise. It has always been our policy to run for cover when it looks like a bad storm and we go off the air as necessary in these circumstances.

"In this case the captain took the decision to head for the high seas and ride it out. He was obviously correct - we're all still here."

The full complement of nine DJs thus shrunk to six but more joined immediately, such was the desire to be a 270 radio star - earning £25 per week.

The new team settles in.

RADIO 270

December 1966

Radio 270 Fun 40 - TOP FIVE

1. Tom Jones - Green Green Grass of Home
2. The Beach Boys - Good Vibrations
3. The Spencer Davis Group - Gimme Some Loving
4. Manfred Mann - Semi-detached Suburban Mr James
5. Lee Dorsey - Holy Cow

Because of the exposed position of the boat during the winter months and the recent damaging publicity, it was decided to move in December to the more sheltered Bridlington Bay. Oceaan 7 was now moored 6 miles from Flamborough Head, 3 and a half miles from Bridlington pier, and 1 mile NE of the South Smithic Buoy. A new marine liaison director was also appointed, the former Whitby Harbourmaster, Captain Frank Graves.

Three new disc jockeys joined at the beginning of the month, replacing those sacked two weeks earlier.

Mike Hayes, 25, came from the Aden Forces' Broadcasting Association. His new show ran from 7pm to 9pm.

24 year old David Sinclair hailed from Orpington and had been assistant station manager and disc jockey with Radio Essex operating from the Knock John fort in the Thames Estuary. David's 270 show ran from 9pm to midnight.

The third of the trio was also from Radio Essex. 18 year old Roger Scott was to present the breakfast show from 6.30 to 9am.

At the end of December popular DJ Pete "Boots" Bowman left the station. He realised the writing was on

Finally On-Air 1966

the wall for the pirates and his London agent found him a job at Radio Montserrat. Although the weather was great Pete disliked the experience, describing the station as "dreadful". He stayed to fulfil his yearlong contract but was determined not to renew it. After returning to the UK he tried for jobs at Radio Luxembourg and Manx, but had no luck and spent a year doing DJ work in dance halls all over the country. He worked for BBC Radio Leeds and also was a DJ at the Mecca Skating Rink in the city. In 1969 he decided to emigrate to Australia, where he stayed initially with Noel and Carole Miller who had also left the station in December. After a year Pete was forced to return to the UK to look after his ailing mother.

Pete "Boots" Bowman.

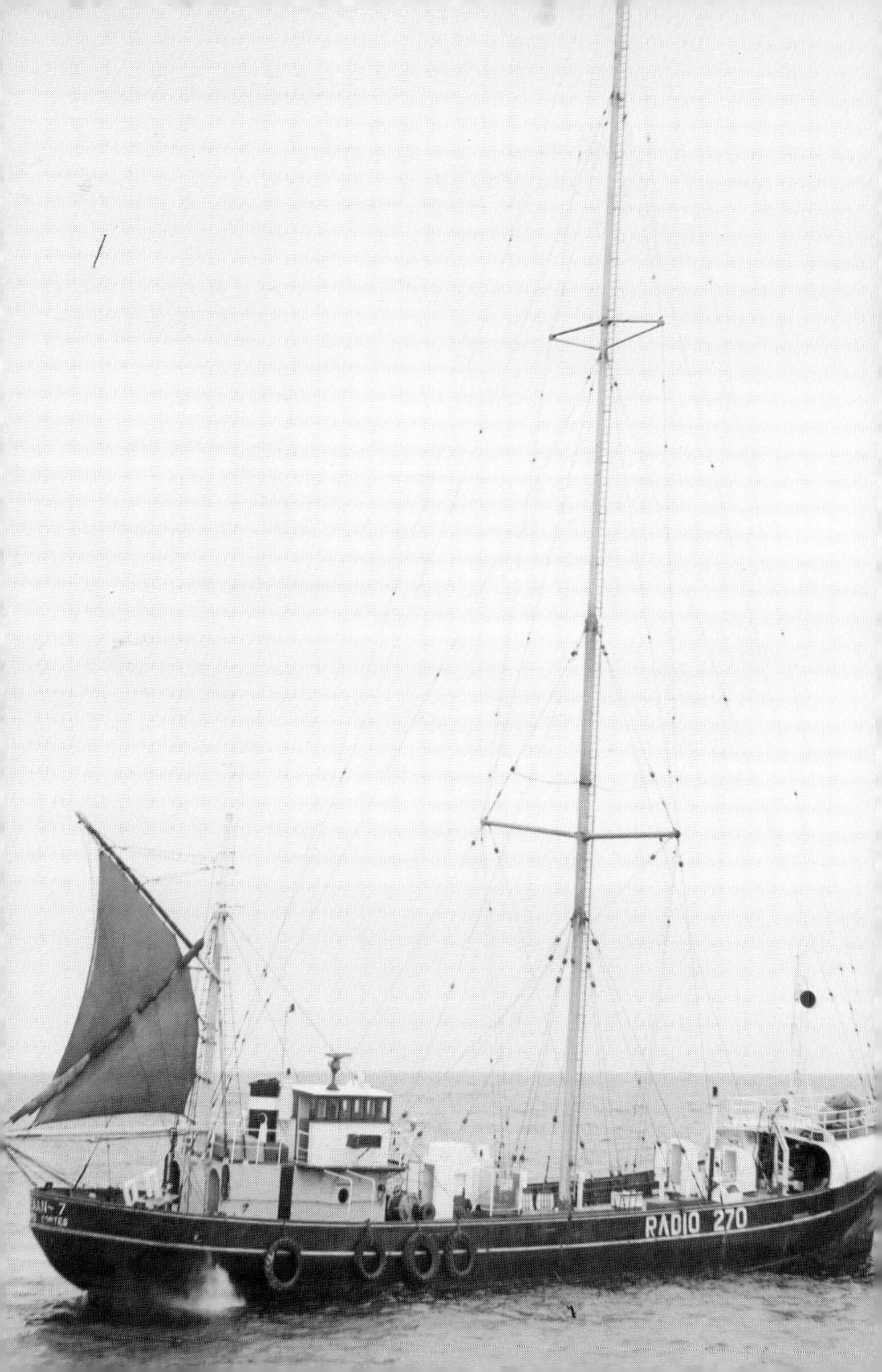
RADIO 270

Chapter Six

On-Air 1967

Radio 270 Fun 40 - TOP FIVE

1. The Seekers - Morning town Ride
2. Donovan - Sunshine Superman
3. Dave Dee, Dozy, Beaky, Mick and Tich - Save Me
4. The Who - Happy Jack
5. The Kinks - Dead End Street

This was the year of the proposed legislation to outlaw the pirate ships - an unsettling time for all the operators.
1967 started successfully for 270 with a full order book of advertising, but behind the scenes some of the formative shareholders tried to remove MD Wilf Proudfoot.

RADIO 270

An extraordinary general meeting was called for Saturday 11th March at the Pavilion Hotel, Scarborough when the following resolution was to be discussed.

It read, "That Wilf Proudfoot be removed from the office of Managing Director without payment of compensation and that removal from office shall take effect forthwith."

The notice convening the meeting had been signed by the original promoters of the station, Don Robinson, Bill Pashby, Peter Duncan, W. H. Steel, M. E. Gardner, and R. E. Hall.

Curiously though just before the meeting Don Robinson and Bill Pashby withdrew their names from the resolution. Both men were invited to propose the resolution but declined. The meeting then gave a vote of confidence in the board and Mr. Proudfoot as managing director. Perhaps it was clear from the impending Marine Offences Bill that to change the direction of the station with only had a few months left was a futile gesture.

For the next five months the battle was on to win hearts and minds in the struggle for a future.

February 1967

From now until the end of broadcasting, staff turnover increased dramatically. Established broadcasters sensed that time was short to secure a future for themselves in the post-pirate era. Many made their way to Radio Luxembourg to gain national exposure and hopefully to be noticed by the bosses at the proposed new BBC pop station. On 270 as each DJ left others were offered short-term contracts, which allowed inexperienced presenters to learn the trade. Many young hopefuls made the phone call to Wilf Proudfoot and were allowed on board at the weekly rate of £12 a week.

March 1967

Radio 270 Fun 40 - TOP FIVE

1. Engelbert Humperdinck - Release Me
2. The Beatles - Penny Lane/Strawberry Fields Forever
3. The Tremeloes - Here Comes My Baby
4. The Monkees - I'm A Believer
5. The Hollies - On a Carousel

DJ Paul Burnett resigned to join Manx Radio in the Isle of Man. He took a pay cut but felt it was time to leave the offshore station before a flood of other jocks were on the search for new job after August. He certainly missed the convenience of taking his blue Mini in for servicing at Tesseyman's garage in Vernon Road during his weeks on board ship. Paul's replacement at 270 was Mark West from Radio Essex, who stayed for 6 months before going to Radio Scotland for the final few months of offshore radio. Mark then became Mark Wesley at Radio Luxembourg.

April 1967

Radio 270 Fun 40 - TOP FIVE

1. Alan Price - Simon Smith and His Amazing Dancing Bear
2. Whistling Jack Smith - I Was Kaiser Bill's Batman
3. Sandie Shaw - Puppet on a String
4. The Seekers - Georgie Girl
5. Frank and Nancy Sinatra - Something Stupid

RADIO 270

At a meeting held by the York Labour Party, on 14th April, the invited speaker was the Postmaster General, Ted Short. Wilf Proudfoot decided to attend and during the discussion he asked if the government would grant his a licence to start a local station for York. The former Tory MP claimed it would cost the BBC £52,000 to run a station in York. He could set up a station for £1,000 and run it for £250 per week.

Naturally Mr. Short declined to issue a licence adding, "We are not yet ready to go forward with local radio. We are not here to help organisations whose primary aim is to make money,"

DJ Bob Snyder joined the station.

May 1967

Radio 270 Fun 40 - TOP FIVE

**1. Jimi Hendrix - Purple Haze
2. The Monkees - A Little Bit Me, A Little Bit You
3. The Move - I Can Hear the Grass Grow
4. The Mamas and Papas - Dedicated to the One I Love
5. Manfred Mann - Ha Ha Said the Clown**

The MP for Haltemprice, Mr Patrick Wall, raised questions in Parliament after hearing an anti-legislation broadcast on Radio 270. Labour MP, Andrew Faulds, also asked the Postmaster General if he would introduce legislation to prevent intervention by illegal radio stations in local or national elections.

Ted Short replied, "It is the first time ever in peacetime that this country has been subjected to a stream of misleading propaganda from outside our territorial waters. I think it is an extremely serious matter and I hope that members who have been dragging their feet about closing down these stations will cease to do so from now on."

Also during May four Tory candidates in the Scarborough local elections paid for advertising time on 270.

DJ Guy Hamilton leaves the station.

June 1967

Radio 270 Fun 40 - TOP FIVE

1. **The Tremeloes - Silence is Golden**
2. **The Kinks - Waterloo Sunset**
3. **Procol Harum - A Whiter Shade of Pale**
4. **The Beach Boys - Then I Kissed Her**
5. **Jimi Hendrix - The Wind Cries Mary**

As foreboding about the imminent legislation increased, religion was seen as a possible salvation of the station. Since 270 began it had taken the half-hour sermons from the American based Church of God. Wilf Proudfoot had seen this as a very

RADIO 270

easy way to keep the station afloat. The income (£1200 each week) from these programmes, which went out at 7.30 every evening, and featured the persuasive voice of Garner Ted Armstrong, had paid all the weekly expenses. The new Marine Offences Bill which was due to have its final reading in the House of Lords this month would make it an offence for any British advertiser to buy air space on the pirates. But if the station accepted foreign advertising there could be little action possible from the government.

The Church of God bought airtime on 280 stations worldwide and was likely to continue its contract with 270 and the other pirates. By reducing the broadcasting time down from 18 to 10 per day and axing many of the 28 staff at 270, the station could survive happily on just this one advertiser. "The DJs don't have to be British citizens - they change their name so often the authorities would have difficulty catching up with them," said Wilf Proudfoot.

These plans though would stay flexible because the aim of 270 was to be allowed ashore properly licensed. Wilf Proudfoot added, "It must come ashore because it is something that 90% of the people want."

More broadsides against the government came from the Conservative Club at York University. Students were offered airtime by Radio 270 and they produced two half-hour programmes of political discussion, both being transmitted at the off peak time of 1.30am on Saturday morning.

The club's Chairman-elect was 20 year old Harvey Proctor who was reading history. He explained, "We have quite a clear conscience about this and we are convinced we are acting within our legal rights."

In the second broadcast, interviews were heard with MP John Biggs-Davison about the Middle East, and with Patrick Wall MP on Rhodesia. Three students also gave short talks, Harvey Proctor on Government and the Individual, Kenneth Garland on Freedom, and Peter Shipley on Patriotism. The theme of the programme was "Land of Hope and Glory."

Also in June an independent candidate in the York local elections bought advertising time on 270. These incidents provoked another Commons question by Kevin MacNamara, MP for Hull North.

He asked about payments for the York University broadcast, which he alleged had aided and abetted the policies of the rebellious regime in Rhodesia. Wilf Proudfoot gave a robust reply, "Mr. MacNamara is talking nonsense. We have invited universities to debate and they have done so. I understand that a group of Young Liberals from York have asked for time and we have agreed to it, and we have done the same for some young communists from Hull."

July 1967

Radio 270 Fun 40 - TOP FIVE

1. The Hollies - Carrie Anne
2. Dave Dee, Dozy, Beaky, Mick and Tich - Okay
3. Traffic - Paper Sun
4. The Turtles - She's Rather Be With Me
5. The Monkees - Alternate Title

A promotion broadcast on 270 in these final few weeks stated the case for commercial radio -

"Progress relies on competition. Television proved this. With the introduction of ITV in 1955 television rapidly improved. Britain is the only democratic country in the world tolerating a monopoly in broadcasting. There is no reason why the BBC and independent commercial radio cannot work side by side to provide a service common to other countries in the free world."

As much as the sentiment matched the times, the promotion rather ignored the fact that every country in Europe also maintained a broadcasting monopoly. It is also a moot point whether, with hindsight, ITV competition had actually improved the quality and range of television programming.

As the new law moved closer Radio 270 had to assess its balance sheet. Wilf Proudfoot revealed the stark figures. "The company owes £20,000 and has payments due from advertisers amounting to £13,000. The reality is that the station will close in debt. At this time no closure date has been announced by the government - it may be within a month or it could drag on to November. If the latter date was reached, the station was likely to at least break even. The best and most practical course for the government was to stop the offshore stations on the day before the new BBC pop station Radio 247 took to the air on September 30th."

The directors of 270 had reservations about the plans by Radio Caroline and Radio London to take American advertising.

Already though, interest was shown in buying the Oceaan 7 as a fully equipped radio station, including two plans, from Newcastle and Leeds, to use the ship as a floating nightclub.

A meeting was called for 26th July when shareholders would be shown the latest financial position and could ask pertinent questions about the board's plans after closure.

Before that meeting though, the government named Monday August 14th as the start date of the new legislation. Wilf Proudfoot put on a brave face and said, "We have not broken the law yet and we do not intend to now. We shall finish broadcasting at 23.59pm on that date. We could recruit a foreign crew and Australian or American DJs, but the bill is full of Thou Shall Nots. When the Bill takes effect presumably we shall not even have letters delivered to our office. This is a comic situation and I think it is a most comic and stupid piece of legislation. The Bill will make it illegal to work for, supply, or advertise on an unregistered station."

"Looking to the future we have a number of possibilities. We could sail the ship up a major river in the North and she could be used as a floating discotheque. We could look into using the vessel in a foreign country and operating from a foreign harbour. Equally we could dismantle and sell the vessel and equipment or we could moor the vessel in harbour and people could pay to look over it." He thought it likely that some of the staff may apply for jobs at the new Yorkshire Television company in Leeds.

RADIO 270

RADIO 270 CLOSES DOWN AFTER 15 MONTHS OF BROADCASTING

RADIO 270, Scarborough's "pirate" radio station, signed off the air for the last time with "Land of Hope and Glory" and "The Queen" on Monday night after 15 months broadcasting.

It was on 14 August, and it would have been more appropriate had it been the thirteenth. Not only was Radio 270 closing down to comply with the Government's Marine Broadcasting (Offences) Act, which came into force at midnight, but

same way as radio stations in any other freedom - loving country.

Appreciation

Mr Dale also thanked the

Chapter Seven

The End of Broadcasting

August 1967

Radio 270 Fun 40 - The Final TOP FIVE

1. The Beatles - All You Need Is Love
2. Scott McKenzie - San Francisco
3. Dave Davies - Death Of A Clown
4. Stevie Wonder - I Was Made To Love Her
5. Pink Floyd - See Emily Play

With just two weeks to go before closedown an air of defiance and desperation descended on all the offshore stations. To lighten the mood, 270 DJ Mike Hayes sent two white carnations to the government - one to Prime Minister, Harold Wilson, and the second to the Postmaster General. The message read, "This country really does need free radio. Love of freedom will prevail." Said DJ Hayes, "It struck me as a psychedelic thought to send the carnations."

On the political front, a third broadside was planned by the York University Monday Club. It was to be transmitted late on Saturday night and will give three Conservative M.P.'s the chance to give their views on the future of commercial radio. Once again Harvey Proctor edited the programme and would offer his views as well. The first two programmes elicited comments in the Commons from the Postmaster General and from two Labour M.P.'s.

RADIO 270

During the final weekend of broadcasting, 270 DJs were on board the pleasure steamer, the Coronia, as the last trips out to the radio ship were made. On the 11th August some lucky youngsters on the Coronia were allowed to talk to DJs via a radiotelephone.

Two farewell balls were held over the weekend in Cleethorpes and Hull. The on-air trailer exhorted, "We want all you mums and dads and kids out there in the wide and wonderful to come along." One newspaper said this was slightly less embarrassing than the usual link heard on pop pirates - "I gotta golden gasser coming up here and it's gonna slay you."

And so listeners tuned in on Monday 14th August to hear the final day of Radio 270. 15 months of broadcasting had made the station a good friend to fans, advertisers and the town of Scarborough, but the North Sea was to have the last word. A ferocious storm blew up and prevented three DJs returning to the station for their final goodbyes. Deputy programme director Mike Hayes, Paul Kramer and Mike Barron did make one attempt to board the ship but were driven back by the waves. In a desperate measure, a helicopter crew from RAF Leconfield flew a sealed bag of taped messages over the ship at 9.15pm - with strict instructions to the programme staff not to mention how the messages had found their way to the station. However the drop was not accurate and the package was lost at sea. Later questions were asked back at base about public money being spent helping the buccaneer pirates. The Prime Minister, Harold Wilson, personally ordered a full enquiry into the RAF's involvement.

On that miserable Monday Captain Olaf Hodgson told a reporter on the Coronia he was determined the sit out the storm for the final day of transmission.

Programme staff remaining on board were Phil Hayton, Ross

The End of Broadcasting

Randell and Rusty Allen. They took it in turn to present the shows, and after Ross's final section finished at 10.30pm, Rusty took over with a nostalgic look back at the past 15 months. He interviewed Captain Hodgson and crew members, Gordon Bailey and Ken Lester. Rusty also recalled many of the household names who had been featured on the 270 airwaves, Noel Miller, Hal Yorke, Paul Burnett, Roger Keene, Boots Bowman and Mark West.

He played farewell messages from DJs past and present. Each said a sincere goodbye followed by their popular theme tunes. At 12 minutes to closedown a letter was read out from the Chairman of Radio 270 Leonard Dale.

"It is very distressing that my company will not be able to provide you with the right kind of radio programme that you have become used to. However the government insists at the present moment to make this form of entertainment illegal when offered by others than the state owned monopoly. We sincerely hope and trust that in the years to come we may have the opportunity of serving you, our listeners, from a land based station. In the fifteen months we have been operating we have tried to give you all the very best in light entertainment and we will attempt to do this again. One must bear in mind that this has cost you nothing and on this our closing day I would like to say a few thank yous. First of all to our many advertisers who have made everything possible. Also I'd like to say thank you to the people of Scarborough and Bridlington and especially those who have helped us in our maritime enterprise. In particular I would like to say thank you to the lifeboat service in Bridlington and also to the air sea rescue organisation from Leconfield who kindly helped us when our captain was taken ill and when we had a small accident to one of our crew members. Furthermore I would like to say a big thank you to all our sea crew both past and present and also to our staff of DJs and engineers and technicians. Finally thank you to our suppliers of foodstuffs and various commodities - we appreciate the cooperation you have given us.

Therefore it is my sorry duty to say goodbye but with the hope that we shall meet again when Britain has free commercial radio like every other freedom loving country.

Signed, Yours sincerely, Leonard H. Dale, Chairman of Radio 270.

Rusty then continued -

And that's it, I also have a telegram, and as you probably know our managing director Mr. Wilf Proudfoot is in Spain right now and unfortunately he couldn't be here with us at the very very end. But I received this telegram from him about two days ago, and it reads, very very short, very very sweetly, "To all Radio 270 listeners and staff, we will return" signed, Wilf Proudfoot, Barcelona.

There you go, what is left, oh dear, it's getting so near the time I don't know whether I'm coming or going. We gonna have another record now and I'll sort something out while we listen to that. And I think this is very very appropriate at this particular time.

The sound of the Roaring Sixties and We Love the Pirate Stations. Six minutes before 12 o'clock, which means we have five minutes, left of broadcasting time. I know we forgot somebody, oh my gosh, and I know it would be tragic if we did. I probably have anyway and I better apologise for that right now whoever I've forgotten, but

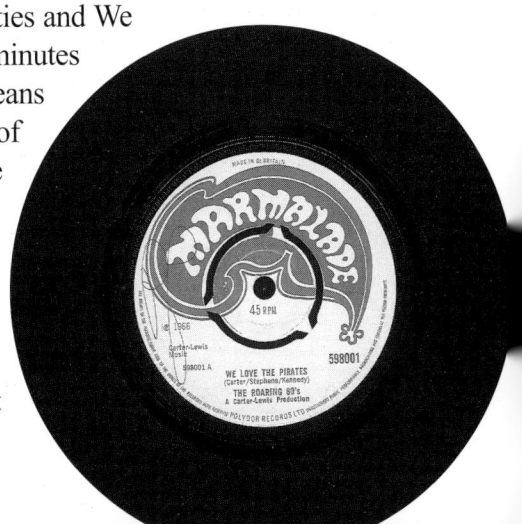

The End of Broadcasting

there's a few people I must just mention. One of course is our chief engineer, the ship's chief engineer on 270, who unfortunately is now in the engine room right now preparing to get the engines ready for us to set sail into Bridlington as soon as we go off the air - that is of course Frankie Dalton, and as I say I'm very very sorry that he couldn't be here to say a few words to you but he does send love to his wife and daughter and he says he'll see you both very very soon and best wishes and love to everybody at Numbers 10 and 16. OK somebody else I must mention, somebody very very important is of course all the shareholders of Radio 270 - I hope you hadn't thought that I'd forgotten you, cause I haven't because you're very very important part and speaking for myself, well no not for myself, for all of us on 270, it's been great working for you all and of course you helped to make everything possible, you helped to make the whole shooting match possible and we really do appreciate it - may I send all of our very very best wishes here on Oceaan 7 to all of you out there, all the shareholders and of course all the directors of 270. And lastly, but by no means least, as they've already been mentioned in Mr. Dale's letter, but I feel I must mention them again, somebody else that's really made this possible, made the 15 months of 270 possible, all the advertisers - all the national and of course all the local advertisers which are just as important. And I hope we've done you some kind of service out there and thank you very very much for your loyalty and for your support, we really do appreciate it.

And that just about winds it up. As I said I think I've thanked everybody for everything and - well that's it - I'm getting a bit - oh boy I think I'm cracking up or something. Five minutes now, that gives us four minutes left - all I've got time to play - one more item.

Disc - Vera Lynn - Land of Hope and Glory

Well we have exactly 60 seconds left, so I haven't said my good-

RADIO 270

byes yet. Well you already know my sentiment. I'm gonna miss you one hell of a lot and from me Rusty, I hope maybe, someday soon in the not too distant future we'll meet on the air again very very soon.

This is Radio 270 broadcasting on 1115 kilocycles in the medium wave band. The time is one and a half minutes before midnight and we're now closing down. On behalf of the 270 men, the radio technicians, the captain and the crew and everybody on shore concerned with Radio 270, this is Rusty Allen wishing you God Bless and God Speed. Goodnight and Goodbye. Radio 270 is now closing down.

Disc - The National Anthem.

At ten past one on Tuesday morning the ship berthed in Bridlington harbour to be met by a group of distraught fans and well wishers. The crew and DJs slept on board and left later in the morning. At 3.30pm the following day Oceaan 7 then left the harbour for her final resting-place in Whitby. A crowd of several hundred holidaymakers met her there as she made her way to the upper harbour where she was finally tied up and mothballed. Captain Hodgson then made his way home to Snainton.

Back in Scarborough DJ Mike Hayes, dressed with an armband over his orange, red and purple shirt led a demonstration in a hairdresser's shop in Dean Road. The beat group, Roll Movement, played to the crowd. Mike Hayes told reporters, "Freedom died in this country last night". After an hour a policeman arrived and the entourage went quietly into the shop and the supporters dispersed. A final Giant Farewell was planned by Mike Hayes and Julian Hewitt for their last UK appearance on Friday 17th November at a dance organised at the Spa Floral Pavilion in Whitby.

Chapter Eight

The End of the Ship - Oceaan 7

Once in Whitby harbour the ship became a major attraction for the many summertime visitors to the resort. Her huge mast dominated all the other vessels in the upper harbour. She was advertised for sale in rather a novel way - a Scarborough estate agent, one of the original shareholders, included her in his weekly listing of houses for sale. The selling price, including all the records, was £12,500.

Enquiries came from interested parties all around the world, including India, Germany, America and Hawaii but the months dragged on before any offer came in.

A shareholders meeting was held at Scarborough's Pavilion

RADIO 270

The Oceaan 7 silent in Whitby's upper harbour.

The End Of the ship-Oceaan 7

Hotel in November and a further one was planned for January when the fully audited accounts would be available.

Offers still came in, according to estate agent, Denys Tuckley. He said in December there was new interest from Australia and Finland. However it was to April 1968 before a definite offer was received - and that was from the Radio Caroline organisation. The price of the ship suddenly doubled to £25,000.

In a dispute over payments their tender company had impounded both Caroline North and South. On the morning of the 3rd March both ships had been forcibly taken off the air and towed back to Amsterdam. Ronan O'Rahilly made attempts to regain control of the boats but was unsuccessful. He then learnt that the Radio 270 ship was still for sale. In secret negotiations he travelled to Whitby to view the ship and to conclude a deal. The Caroline crew booked in to the Hayburn Wyke Hotel, at Cloughton, however all these plans were leaked prematurely to a national newspaper and the Scarborough directors were informed they would be prosecuted if they allowed the ship out of harbour.

The Caroline plan was to take the ship and moor her off Frinton. A DJ crew was lined up to include Don Allen, Roger Day, Andy Archer, Jim Gordon, Freddie Beare and Roger Scott. Roger Day even received a telephone call at his London flat saying get to Whitby and be ready to sail out that evening!

No more offers came in after this warning from the government and to prove Oceaan 7 could never again broadcast, her 154ft aerial was removed on 16th September 1968.

The marine superintendent of the redundant ship was still Captain Frank Graves, the former Whitby harbourmaster. Each week he inspected the ship and the moorings while the engines were started by Frank Dalton who had also worked on the ship during her broadcasting days.

In early October the Northern Echo printed this advert-

RADIO 270

"Radio 270, Radio and Ship equipment for sale. Ring Scarborough 63638/9 for details."

Office manageress, Stella Ellis, explained the law made it an offence to sell a ship for broadcasting purposes, so the Oceaan 7 had been stripped of her radio equipment to sell separately.

Various souvenirs were sold - the Angel Hotel in Whitby bought the barometer, ships clock and lifebelt. Another lifebuoy went to the Empire Cafe. Wilf Proudfoot kept the tape recorders and 270 jingle tapes as a memento. Later the Ship's Log (distance recorder), lifebelt and Course Corrector were donated to the Maritime Museum at Hartlepool. All the Top 40 discs, albums and grams were given to Scarborough Hospital Radio service.

By the end of October a sale of the ship had been concluded. Scrap dealer T.Smith and Son of Hartlepool bought her. At 8am on Sunday 27th October Frankie Dalton piloted her out of Whitby under the ship's own steam - although an escort was provided to comply with the law.

After languishing in the Coal Dock in West Hartlepool for a few months she was finally sold to the ship breakers, Hughes Bolckow of Blyth. They purchased her for £1,350 on the 6th February 1969 and she was towed to their shipyard on the 11th. Demolition commenced on the 17th February and was completed by the 29th March, resulting in a profit for the company of £376. The ship's wheel was bought from Blyth for £17.50 by former 270 shareholder and technical director Peter Duncan.

But this was not quite the end. The powerful and expensive transmitter was stored in the basement of Wilf Proudfoot's home in Scalby Road. There is lay for a few years before being bought for use on another offshore station.

Paul Harris, author of a number of books about pirate stations, was involved in the planning for Capital Radio in late 1969 and the station finally began testing on 270 metres in April 1970.

The End Of the ship-Oceaan 7

However technical and maritime problems dogged the fledgling station and the project was abandoned by November. Paul Harris revealed to me that he had paid £1200 for the transmitter and after the project was abandoned many of the parts were removed and the transmitter broken up prior to the scrapping of their vessel.

TUCKLEY AND CO

DT/JB/144

D. van Schenk Brill, Esq.,
Kleverlaan 112 A,
Haarlam,
Holland.

16 Pavilion Square
Scarborough
Telephone
Scarborough 5352

Principals
P. Home Tuckley B.A.
Denys Tuckley

Estate Agents
Valuers
Auctioneers
Land Agents

20th March, 1968.

Dear Sir,

Re: Seaborne Radio Station - Radio 270 - Ship Oceaan VII

Thank you for your kind enquiry of 11th March and addressed to our Whitby Office. We hasten to enclose the details of the ship which you have requested, and these details, of course, include the equipment which is installed therein.

The asking price for the ship is £25,000 at Whitby. This price is to include all the equipment and furnishings installed in the ship as per the enclosed details. We understand from the Chairman of the Company, Ellambar Investments Limited, which own the ship, that all the equipment, motors, engines, etc. are in good working order; the ship is in a good seaworthy condition and could be sailed out of Whitby on any tide. We know that all the engines and equipment have been tested and run for a short time every Thursday since the ship has been berthed in Whitby as an engineer has spent each Thursday morning checking all the working parts.

Concerning the matter of commission if you succeed in selling the ship for us. We are quite prepared to allow you half of our commission after we have deducted our advertising expenses. Our commission rate has been fixed by the Company at 3% of the sale price, therefore, on £25,000 this would amount to £750. Our advertising expenses todate amount to £150. In the event of you obtaining a sale to a willing and able buyer who has not been introduced to the ship already from any source, your share of commission would be £300.

We should be glad to make arrangements for your applicants to view this ship at any time that is suitable to them, and we await hearing of your further interest.

Yours faithfully,

Denys Tuckley.

P.S. Would you kindly return the artist's copy of Oceaan VII after perusal?

Replying to a sale enquiry from Holland.

Chapter Nine

The Dream of Land-Based Commercial Radio

Wilf Proudfoot never gave up in his desire to see commercial radio for Scarborough become a reality. A couple of years after the closure of 270 and five days after Yorkshire Television went to colour, he set up a small company, East Yorkshire Radio Ltd. This was registered with capital of £500 in £1 shares and had as the directors the familiar names of Wilf Proudfoot, Peter Asquith, Tim Jackson, Roland Hill and Anthony Rylands - all ex-270 directors.

Six months later the group bought the old Admiralty base just outside Scarborough off Racecourse Hill, opposite the existing signals station. Conveniently this site came complete with four 50ft high transmitter masts. The group proposed starting a station immediately and boasted it could be opened on a shoestring. In fact they said it would cost only £1000, have a staff of three and be on the air within two weeks. This compares favourably with the stated cost of £60,000 for a BBC local station and £100,000 annual running costs.

At the same time Wilf Proudfoot returned to the House of Commons as MP for Brighouse and in 1971 he was asked to attend the Standing Committee considering the Tory proposals for UK commercial radio. His tenure with this committee undoubtedly shows Wilf Proudfoot to be a pioneering architect in the introduction of legal commercial radio in the UK.

His long held dream of a land-based station in Scarborough finally came to fruition when Yorkshire

RADIO 270

Coast Radio launched in November 1993. This commercial station based in Scarborough was originally to be housed on a trawler in the harbour. The "Hatherleigh" was owned by Tom Pindar, Chairman of YCR. The trawler would also double as a floating maritime museum.

However after a shareholders meeting in May it was decided to distance themselves from a "pirate" image and be housed in the more conventional surroundings of the old TSB Bank building in Falsgrave Road.

The station manager for the Sunday 7th November launch was Jerry Scott, a one-time pirate with Radio Caroline, and now the afternoon show presenter on BBC Radio York.

Wilf Proudfoot naturally was a founding shareholder in Yorkshire Coast Radio which has gone on to become a hugely successful local station. But with a set-up cost of £250,000, Wilf's early assessment of local radio in the seventies, was correct - significant profits are virtually impossible at this level of investment.

Other major shareholders included Paul Rusling, Barry Robinson, Sarah McCarthy, and Tim Jackson. Wilf and his two sons are also shareholders in Paul Rusling's new national station, Music Mann 279, soon to be launched on Long Wave from the Isle of Man - with its massive transmitter in Ramsey Bay - the 60's base for Radio Caroline North.

As a postscript to Radio 270, a piece of history was rediscovered in November 1989 when fishermen aboard the trawler, "Success" caught a 30ft section of the Radio 270 transmitter mast in their nets. The aluminium mast was brought ashore and sold for scrap. Although the station was only on the air for 15 months, its ghost is forever present on the East Coast!

Bill Pashby died February 1975.
Leonard Dale died February 1986.
Stella Ellis now lives in Spain.
Maggie Lucas, the 270 Set organiser, lives in Australia.
Peter Duncan later Chief Engineer at Liverpool's Radio City is now retired and lives on a canal boat.
Don Robinson's enterprises continued. He opened Mr Marvels Amusement Park on the North Bay, he successfully ran the Opera House Theatre, he was a director of Trident Television and latterly Chairman of Hull Kingston Rovers. He owned farms in Bulgaria and is now a local Councillor in Scarborough.
Wilf Proudfoot lives in Scarborough where he runs his long established supermarket business. He is a shareholder in both Yorkshire Coast Radio and the new Isle of Man long wave station, Music Mann 279. He is also a trained hypnotist.

RADIO 270

Chapter Ten

The 270 DJ's - Where Are They Now?

The magic of radio is that the DJ voices you hear every day eventually become like a friend. You learn all about their interests, passions, dislikes and frustrations. Many listeners wrote to their favourite presenters and started a sort of pen friend relationship. And when a DJ decides the time is right to leave the station - or if he's fired, then for the loyal listener, it really is like losing a genuine friend. So for memories of those long lost friends, this is the reminder of the DJs on board Radio 270, and as far is possible we also list where they are now and what they're up to in their life after being a star on the ocean radio waves.

Vince "Rusty" Allen. Born 1937. Vince joined a little station on a fort in the Thames estuary, Radio Essex in 1965, eventually becoming an executive. After learning his trade there he came to Scarborough in April 1967 as 270 joint Programme Controller. He stayed until the very end and presented the close down show on August 14th. He never worked in radio again and was last heard of being employed by Southend council. His hobby is studying railway history. His 270 theme tune, Deep in the Heart of Texas, Duane Eddy.

John Aston. He was only on the station for a short time and left in April 1967 to join a new station Radio 355 on the old Swinging Radio England/Britain Radio boat in the south. He now works in the film industry.

Mike Barron. When Radio Essex closed in October 1966, Mike came to 270. He stayed until the end and then went on to work as a continuity announcer at various TV stations including Tyne Tees. He died in the 1990's.

The 270 DJ's - Where Are They Now ?

Pete "Boots" Bowman. Born 1944. Pete began his radio career with Radio Scotland where he worked with Roger Gale. He met up again with Roger at 270 and stayed until the end of 1966. His nickname came from the leather cowboy boots he often wore. His pay cheque was even made out to B. Bowman. After 270 he went to Radio Montserrat, then to Australia, and eventually back to the UK where in the 1980's he worked for Trust House Forte Hotels in London. His 270 theme tune, Bird Rocker by the Ventures.

Paul Burnett. Born 1943. Paul was the first DJ to be signed up to 270. Don Robinson had become aware of him after a newspaper article spotlighted Paul's DJ work at the Top Rank in Darlington. He was in the RAF at the time and had to pay £125 to buy himself out of the service. Paul hosted the 270 Breakfast show, as well as an early evening show. After leaving 270 he took £10 pay cut and went to Manx Radio on the Isle of Man - at the time the UK's only legal land based station. From here he was heard on Luxembourg and eventually BBC Radio One. These days he's a presenter on the Classic Gold Network. His 270 theme tune, Perfidia by Bob Miller and the Millermen.

Alex Dee. Born 1944. Alex enjoyed a year at Radio City from 1965 until he joined 270 the following year. In November 1966, Alex, 20, was fired by the station for talking to the press about conditions on board the tender boat. Later he worked for a number of the new BBC local stations. He was last heard of working as a shop assistant.

Roger Gale. A direct descendant of Sir Francis Drake, Roger acquired his experience of radio broadcasting by being on Radio Caroline North from August 1964, later transferring to the Caroline South ship.

RADIO 270

From there it was north to Radio Scotland as Programme Director. He joined 270 for the start in April 1966 and was the first voice on the station when it eventually launched in June. His stay in Scarborough was short-lived and he later worked for BBC Radio London and as a presenter on TV's Magpie programme. He is now the long serving Conservative MP for North Thanet. On 270 his theme tune was A Walk in the Black Forest by Horst Jankowski.

Roger Keene. Described as a real smoothy, Roger (real name Roger Gomez) used to be press officer and road manager for the ex-Shadows bass player, Jet Harris. Roger joined 270 in 1966 and immediately made a great impression on the ladies. His theme tune was Cats Squirrel by Cream. From 270 he travelled and worked in radio in Canada, where he died in 1988.

Guy Hamilton. Joining Radio Essex in July 1966 Guy was there until January 1967 when he came aboard Radio 270. His stay was only for three months but he was persuaded back for a number of short trips during the summer. Guy, real name Gerry Zierler, now runs a very successful TV airtime sales organisation, Zierler Media.

Mike Hayes. Gaining his experience during his time in the RAF at Aden Forces Broadcasting, Mike then joined 270 in 1967 and stayed to the end. He then travelled and worked in Germany and is now retired and living in Holland. His 270 theme tune, There's a Rainbow around my Shoulder - the Ted Heath Orchestra.

Phil Hayton. Joined 270 as a newsreader in spring 1967 on £8 per week. One day all the jocks were seasick and Phil broadcast for the whole day. Phil's 270 theme tune was Countdown by Dave "Baby" Cortez. He was with the station right to the end

The 270 DJ's - Where Are They Now ?

after which he worked for BBC Radio Leeds. He now presents the news on BBC World TV.

Allen Ives. 18 year old Allen, from Romford in Essex, was aboard the ship for the opening day. He also experienced the appalling gale the next night. He never broadcast on the station, leaving shortly afterwards and not returning for the launch in June.

Jeff Jones. Jeff also joined in late spring 1967 - mainly reading the news. He is now a presenter at Moray Firth Radio in Aberdeen.

Andy Kirk. Born 1947. Andy was the youngest DJ to join 270 and was appointed before the station went on air. He lived in Collingham near Wetherby before joining the station, and was one of the three DJs fired in November 1966. After this he set up a business in Leeds, where he still lives and is a near neighbour of Sir Jimmy Savile.

Paul Kramer. Born 1947. A one-time film recording engineer, Paul was with Radio City from July 1966 until February 1967 after which he joined 270.

Noel Miller. Born 1944. Australian "Neddy" Noel was appointed Programme Controller when the station finally began broadcasting in June 1966. After he left he went back to Australia and worked in the family catering business. He continued presenting radio shows in his spare time, later going full time as the breakfast presenter on Fox FM between 1981 to 1986. He then worked part time on various stations but quit radio in 1990 to lead a more stable existence and concentrate on his catering career as a chef.

RADIO 270

Ed Moreno. Born 1931. Although born in England, Ed spent his early years in America. His radio work took him to Hong Kong, Japan and the American Forces Network in Germany. Back in England he joined Radio Invicta in 1964 followed by Radio City in 1966, then to 270 in 1967 as joint Programme Controller with Rusty Allan, staying with the station until closedown in August. After this he trained as a doctor and went in General Practice. After suffering severe depression he committed suicide in 1980, aged 47.

Brendan Power. Initially turned down by Noel Miller, but when Noel left, Brendan called Wilf Proudfoot and said he had been hired and when should he start. Luckily there was a vacancy, Pete Bowman had just left, and Brendan began on 270 in late December 1965. He only stayed a few months before following Pete Bowman to Radio Montserrat. He was back in the UK in 1973 when he joined a station in Birmingham. Now he works in financial services and is a motivational speaker. His theme tune was Rockin' Goose by Johnny and the Hurricanes.

Roger Scott. Another presenter from Radio Essex, Roger's stay on 270 was fairly short-lived before he went to the easy-listening station Radio 390. He joined Caroline North just four days before the ship was taken off-air and towed back to Holland in 1968. In 1972 Roger was on Radio North Sea under the name of Arnold Layne. He is now a freelance broadcaster known as Greg Bance.

David Sinclair. Following a similar career path as Roger Scott - from Radio Essex to 270, and then back down south to Radio 390. David, now in Canada, owns a music publishing company and also runs voice courses.

The 270 DJ's - Where Are They Now ?

Dennis Straney. Born 1941. From the Essex station on a fort, Radio City, Dennis came to 270 in June 1966 just in time for the launch. He became a 270 favourite as "Dennis the Menace" although not with the management who fired him, but quickly reinstated him, following protests from listeners. Eventually Dennis went back to Australia where he worked initially as a store demonstrator. He is now believed to be selling insurance. On 270 he opened his show with the theme tune, "On the Street Where You Live" by the David Stacey Orchestra.

Leon Tipler. Born 1943. Joining 270 from Radio City, Leon presented the Breakfast show on alternate weeks with Paul Burnett. He freelanced in radio after leaving 270 and was on the Belgian pirate, Radio Atlantis in 1974. He is now a commercial producer and voice-over man in Shropshire.

Alan West. Born 1947. Better known on 270 as Ross Randall, he was with the station until the very last day. He then went to BBC local stations and eventually back on the ocean waves with Radio North Sea. He is now the project manager on a community station in South London.

Mark West. Mark was once in a band, managed by Rusty Allen, who introduced Mark to the world of Radio Essex. Joining 270 shortly after Rusty, Mark replaced Paul Burnett and stayed with the station for three months before moving further north to Radio Scotland. He changed his name to Mark Wesley when he joined Radio Luxembourg. He now runs his own production company.

RADIO 270

Hal Yorke. Born 1941. BBC trained Hal was second in command and studio manager at 270 where he presented the afternoon show. After this he went to Radio Hong Kong producing dramas then running his own theatre company. He now owns a web design company in Hong Kong where he works under his real name, Norman Wingrove. His 270 theme tune was Man of Mystery by the Shadows.

Other broadcasting staff on Radio 270 were **Robin Best, Stacey Brewer, Bob Dewing, Albert Hart, Julian Hewitt, Roger King, Mick the Mod, Bob Snyder and Steve Taylor.** American **Ben Toney** was a radio consultant during late March and April 1966, before joining Swinging Radio England, which went on air in May.

The Pirate Hall of Fame website is highly recommended and updates on a monthly basis the whereabouts of all the offshore radio broadcasters.

The UK's Beat Fleet - Floating Offshore Radio 1964 - 1967

March 1964	Radio Caroline
May 1964	Radio Atlanta
July 1964	Radio Atlanta merges with Caroline and sails to the Isle of Man as Caroline North.
December 1964	Radio London
January 1966	Radio Scotland
May 1966	Swinging Radio England/Britain Radio
June 1966	Radio 270

About the Author

Sadly too young to have worked aboard the offshore stations, the author has always been fascinated by music and radio.

He began his career with the BBC in the early seventies as a cameraman working on such diverse programmes as Top of the Pops, Panorama and Jackanory. He learnt his radio craft at BBC Radio London, and after a short time as cameraman on the Old Grey Whistle Test he came north to Yorkshire Television.

After a chance meeting with Keith Skues in the YTV bar he was offered freelance shows at Radio Hallam in Sheffield. Other commercial stations he has broadcast on include Pennine Radio, Radio Tees, Radio Aire, and Magic 828.

He started presenting country shows on the BBC, first at Radio Humberside, followed by BBC Radio York where he can be heard presenting "Hot Country" every Saturday evening 9pm to midnight. BBC Radios Sheffield, Leeds and Humberside also broadcast the show.

Back in television he is a Continuity Announcer for Yorkshire, Tyne Tees, Granada and Border.

Between 1984 and 1992 he ran the Castle Cinema in Pickering and since 1994 has owned the Wetherby Film Theatre.

His numerous books include two on the history of Roller Coasters and seven on Yorkshire cinemas and theatres. Recently he has completed books on West Yorkshire, Ilkley and Yorkshire for the Francis Frith Collection.

RADIO 270

Acknowledgements.

My thanks to Bryan Berryman and his team at the Scarborough Library. Help was also offered by radio experts Carl Kingston, Graham L. Hall and Paul Rusling.

Many shareholders and directors were happy to tell me about their part in the jigsaw. Perhaps surprising though some DJs were initially reluctant to recall their time at the station.

Photographs came from many sources over the years. Some were sent to Carl Kingston while he was on Radio Caroline's Ross Revenge. It is impossible to name the original photographers. If any copyright has been inadvertently infringed, this will be corrected in the next edition.